GREAT WESTERN
LARGE-WHEELED OUTSIDE-FRAMED 4-4-0 TENDER LOCOMOTIVES

GREAT WESTERN

LARGE-WHEELED OUTSIDE-FRAMED 4-4-0 TENDER LOCOMOTIVES

ATBARA, BADMINTON, CITY AND FLOWER CLASSES

by

DAVID MAIDMENT

PEN & SWORD
TRANSPORT

First published in Great Britain in 2017 by
Pen & Sword Transport

An imprint of Pen & Sword Books Ltd
47 Church Street, Barnsley, South Yorkshire S70 2AS

ISBN 978 1 52670 095 7

Pen & Sword Books Ltd incorporates the imprints of Pen & Sword
Archaeology, Atlas, Aviation, Battleground, Discovery, Family History,
History, Maritime, Military, Naval, Politics, Railways, Select, Social History,
Transport, True Crime, and Claymore Press, Frontline Books, Leo Cooper,
Praetorian Press, Remember When, Seaforth Publishing and Wharncliffe.

For a complete list of Pen & Sword titles please contact
Pen & Sword Books Limited
47 Church Street, Barnsley, South Yorkshire S70 2AS England
E-mail: enquiries@pen-and-sword.co.uk
Website: www.pen-and-sword.co.uk

Design and typesetting
by Juliet Arthur, www.stimula.co.uk

Printed and bound in China by Imago

All David Maidment's royalties from this book will be donated to the
Railway Children charity [reg. no. 1058991] [www.railwaychildren.org.uk]

CONTENTS

Other books by David Maidment:
Novels (Religious historical fiction)
The Child Madonna, Melrose Books, 2009
The Missing Madonna, PublishNation, 2012
The Madonna and Her Sons, PublishNation, 2015

Novels (Railway fiction)
Lives on the Line, Max Books, 2013

Non-fiction (Railways)
The Toss of a Coin, PublishNation, 2014
A Privileged Journey, Pen and Sword, 2015
An Indian Summer of Steam, Pen and Sword, 2015
Great Western Eight-Coupled Heavy Freight Locomotives, Pen and Sword, 2015
Great Western Moguls and Prairies, Pen and Sword, 2016
The Urie and Maunsell 2-cylinder 4-6-0s, Pen and Sword, 2016
Great Western Small-Wheeled Double-Framed 4-4-0s, Pen & Sword, 2017
The Development of the German Pacific Locomotive, Pen & Sword 2017

Non-fiction (Street Children)
The Other Railway Children, PublishNation, 2012
Nobody ever listened to me, PublishNation, 2012

PREFACE

This is the second 'Pen and Sword' locomotive portfolio about Great Western double-framed 4-4-0s that emerged at a critical changeover period with William Dean overlapping with George Jackson Churchward at the helm of GW locomotive design and practice. The previous volume covered the mixed traffic engines with 5ft 8in coupled wheels – primarily the 'Dukes' and 'Bulldogs', designed initially for passenger work in Devon and Cornwall after the conversion of the last broad gauge route, before multiplying as the all-purpose secondary engines all over the system. The Dean/Churchward combination also tackled the need for express passenger locomotives required to haul the heavier loads being encountered at the turn of the century, and the 6ft 8in 4-4-0s emerged from Swindon Works at the same time – the 'Badminton's of 1898, the 'Atbaras' of 1900, the 'Cities' of 1903 and finally the 'Flowers' of 1908.

In that first decade of the century these locomotives made a huge impact, but within that same period train loads increased significantly again, so that Churchward's standard express passenger 4-6-0 designs made their domination of GW express traffic short-lived. The later standardisation by Collett building on Churchward's policies made them all superfluous by the late 1920s, with all being withdrawn by the early 1930s with just one example preserved, the celebrated 3440 *City of Truro*.

I am therefore very reliant on previous transport historians and the libraries and photographic archives of the Great Western Trust at Didcot, the Manchester Locomotive Society in Stockport and the Model Railway Club at Kings Cross, for both text and photos. In particular I have valued the RCTS GW locomotive history books and the two volumes of O.S. Nock's books on the subject written in the 1970s and published by David & Charles. Access to early copies of the *Railway Magazine* and the locomotive performance articles by Charles Rous-Marten and Cecil J. Allen at the MLS library has been very useful and helped to flush out a rounded picture of the performance of these engines on the road. The Society photographic archives have been a mine of mostly previously unpublished photographs and have been extremely valuable. Finding the best photos has been facilitated by Laurence Waters at the GW Trust Archive and Paul Shackcloth at MLS in particular, and I owe them, and Mike Bentley for making available his personal collection, a great debt of gratitude. Not only have they made the splendid photos available but have allowed me to use them free of any publication charge or at a significantly reduced fee, as again the royalties are being donated to Railway Children, the charity I founded in 1995 to support street children at transport terminals in India and East Africa and runaway children in the United Kingdom.

Last and by no means least, I acknowledge the constant support and help from the Pen and Sword staff, particularly John Scott-Morgan, Transport Commissioning Editor, Carol Trow, the editor of my books, Juliet Arthur, the book designer, and Jodie Butterwood and Janet Brookes who had overall editorial and production responsibilities for the 'Locomotive Portfolio' series and other transport history books.

David Maidment
September 2016

CHAPTER 1

THE 'ARMSTRONGS'
DESIGN & CONSTRUCTION

Dean's 1884 7ft 8in 2-2-2 rebuild of the unsuccessful 4-2-4T, No, 9. (GW Trust)

The Great Western Railway's final conversion of broad to standard gauge was undertaken in the West of England and was completed by May 1892. The first track rebuilding to standard gauge took place in the 1860s and locomotives for both broad and standard gauges were being produced simultaneously by the GWR engineering works at Swindon and Wolverhampton. William Dean succeeded Joseph Armstrong as Chief Locomotive, Carriage and Wagon Superintendent at Swindon in 1877, whilst George Armstrong managed the construction of standard gauge locomotives at the Stafford Road Wolverhampton Works until 1892. Dean was in charge of design and production of locomotives for both broad and standard gauges from his appointment at Swindon. His most significant designs until the late 1880s were the long-lived 'Dean Goods' 0-6-0s of 1883 and his substantial improvements in rolling stock. Little development of locomotives for the broad gauge took place as its demise was imminent.

In 1881, he had built a curious standard gauge 4-2-4T with 7ft 8in driving wheels which did little work as it was prone to derailments – he rebuilt it as a 2-2-2 tender engine with 18in x 26in cylinders in 1884. In the mid 1880s, he experimented with the design of a number of engines intended for passenger work. No.7 was a 7ft 0½ in wheeled 2-4-0 compound locomotive built in 1886 for the standard gauge with 23in low pressure cylinders, but it ran few miles, was difficult to maintain because of its inaccessible inside motion and was laid aside in 1890. No.8 was of similar design to No.7 but ran on the broad gauge as a 'convertible'. However, it suffered from the same defects as No.7 and never entered regular service.

The rebuilt 4-2-4T, then a 2-2-2, was given the number,'9', and after a chequered career, was rebuilt again in 1890 to the successful Joseph Armstrong 'Queen' 2-2-2 class, and named 'Victoria'. These standard gauge 2-2-2s had been built between 1873 and 1875 with 7ft single driving wheels and 18in x 24in cylinders and had operated successfully on the main standard gauge routes to Swindon and Gloucester and to Wolverhampton via Oxford. They

were withdrawn between 1903 and the start of the First World War in 1914, most of them running over a million miles in traffic.

Then, in 1886, he built an important engine, a 2-2-2 , No.10, with 7ft 8in driving and 4ft 6in front and rear carrying wheels, intending to equip it with Joy's valve gear. However, No.9, before rebuilding as a 'Queen' class, was having problems with this gear, and Dean therefore built No.10 with slide valves located under the cylinders and Stephenson's link motion, a piece of machinery invented by Stroudley on the London Brighton &

No.9, further rebuilt in 1890 and named *Victoria* in line with Joseph Armstrong's 7ft diameter 2-2-2 express passenger locomotive No.55 *Queen* which gave its name to the class. (GW Trust)

No.9 at work, piloted by a Joseph Armstrong 2-2-2 No.158, on an express at West Drayton, c.1900. (GW Trust)

As built in 1886, Dean's 2-2-2 No.10, the prototype Dean 7ft 8½ in express engine using the Stroudley designed valves and arrangement of the Stephenson link motion that became a standard element of the later Dean 4-4-0 locomotives. (GW Trust)

South Coast Railway. This was the first GW locomotive with that valve gear and motion, which Dean then applied to his subsequent designs. Dean also increased the maximum travel of the valves of the Stephenson link motion from Stroudley's and Holden's 3⅞in to 4⅝in with generous port openings as the gear was linked up – this seems to have been one of the factors that gave Dean's express engines their reputation for speed (though for some reason evaded in the rebuilding of the four 'Armstrongs' to be discussed in a few paragraphs'

time). He reconstructed No.10 in 1890 with 7ft instead of the larger diameter single driving wheels, in similar fashion to No.9 and the 'Queen' class and the rebuilt locomotive was named 'Royal Albert'. It was withdrawn from service in 1906. In 1888, Dean built two further experimental 2-4-0s for the Broad Gauge, but as 'convertibles', both of more conventional 'simple' rather than compound steam propulsion, numbered 14 and 16.

Dean was, however, developing the 2-2-2 wheel arrangement for his express passenger engines, similar in general arrangement to the Joseph Armstrong 2-2-2s. His first production passenger engines, using the valve gear concepts he had developed on No.10, were large wheeled 'singles', 2-2-2s, numbered 3000-3030, built in 1891-2. 3021-3028

A further photo in traffic of Dean's 2-2-2 No.10 with 7ft 8½ in driving wheels as built, c.1889. (GW Trust)

Dean's reconstruction of No. 10 in 1890 in similar form to the Joseph Armstrong 'Queen' class with 7ft driving wheel, and named *Royal Albert*.
(GW Trust)

A further photo of No. 10 in traffic at Swindon station, c.1895.
(GW Trust)

No.10 *Royal Albert,* in its final rebuilt form as a 7ft 2-2-2 of the 'Queen' class, at Swindon, 24 May 1905. (GW Trust)

No.10 *Royal Albert* in action, seen here on a down express near Acton, c.1900. (GW Trust)

The 1886 built Dean 'compound' 2-4-0, No.8, in original condition. (MLS Collection)

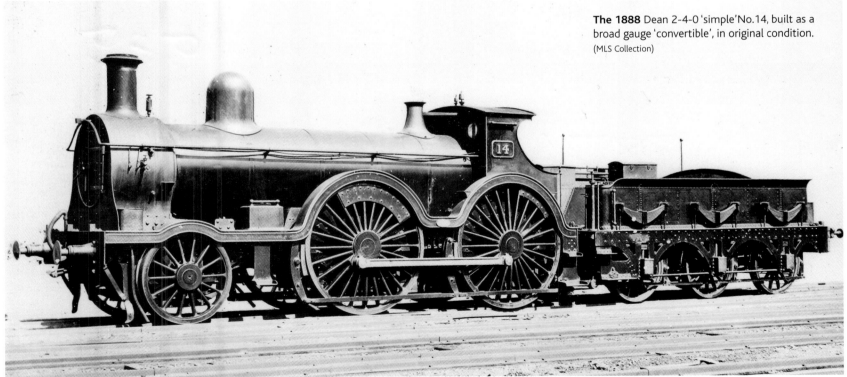

The 1888 Dean 2-4-0 'simple' No.14, built as a broad gauge 'convertible', in original condition. (MLS Collection)

Dean 2-2-2 'convertible', 3028, one of eight (3021-28) built for the broad gauge in August 1891, utilising the valve gear developed on No.10, and converted to standard gauge in August 1892 and rebuilt again as a 4-2-2 and named *Wellington*. (MLS Collection)

Another view of a Dean 2-2-2 'convertible', 3024, also later converted to a standard gauge 2-2-2 and to a 4-2-2 'Dean Single'. (MLS Collection)

The Dean 2-2-2 converted to standard gauge, 3021 *Wigmore Castle* in works grey, c.1892. This was the locomotive that derailed at speed at Box and was, with its sisters, then rebuilt as a 4-2-2. (GW Trust)

One of the converted broad gauge 2-2-2s , No.3026 *Tornado* in traffic. Its frame and tender have been 'guivered' with tallow, a practice favoured and requested by some drivers of that time, c.1900. (GW Trust)

Dean 'Single' 2-2-2, No.3006 *Courier*, c.1895. (MLS Collection)

were actually constructed as broad gauge 'convertibles' and were indeed rebuilt for the standard gauge in 1892. 3000-3020 and 3029-30 were built for the standard gauge.

They were fast locomotives but one, 3021 *Wigmore Castle*, became derailed at speed in Box Tunnel in September 1893 with a large number of fatalities and injuries. Their stability at speed with only a pony truck to guide came under investigation and despite his reluctance to countenance four

wheel bogies at the front end, Dean started to consider the use of a four-wheel bogie truck. At the works and doing little work because of the problems they had encountered were the four 2-4-0s, three broad gauge 'convertibles' and one standard gauge, numbers 7, 8, 14 and 16.

Dean overcame his prejudice against four-wheel front bogies and rebuilt these four engines completely in 1894 as standard gauge 4-4-0s with 7ft 1in coupled wheels and large 20in x 26in stroke cylinders.

The boiler had 1,561.33sqft of heating surface, was pressed at 160lbpsi and the grate area was 20.8sqft. The axle-weight on the driving wheel was just under 16 tons, and the engine weight was 50 tons 16 cwt with a six-wheel tender weighing 36 tons 15 cwt., and having water capacity of 3,000 gallons. Tractive effort at 85% was 16,640lb. They were handsome locomotives, known as the 'Armstrong' class after the name bestowed to No.7, but were disappointing on the road. One

No.7 *Charles Saunders* as rebuilt in 1894 and subsequently renamed *Armstrong*. The name 'Charles Saunders' was transferred to No.14. The photo was taken in the 1890s prior to the renaming.
(Bob Miller/MLS Collection)

Former Dean broad gauge compound 2-4-0 No.8, rebuilt by Dean as a 7ft 1in 4-4-0 in 1894 and named *Gooch*.
(Bob Miller/MLS Collection)

4-4-0 No.7 renamed *Armstrong*, at Swindon, c.1900. (GW Trust)

No.7 *Armstrong* rebuilt from standard gauge 2-4-0 Compound in 1894, at Swindon, before being rebuilt with a cone boiler, c.1900.
(Bob Miller/MLS Collection)

theory was that their 20in diameter cylinders were too large for the boiler, causing them to become 'breathless' on the long level lines of the GW's main routes and new 19in cylinders were fitted in 1903-4. Their livery was lined GW green, crimson lake splashers and underframes. The names were raised brass letters on the splashers and numbers were large brass figures on the cab sides.

With the successful bogie conversions and the 1895 experience of the Box Tunnel derailment of his express 2-2-2, and the experience of the use of the bogies on the four locomotives of the 'Armstrong' class,

No. 14 *Charles Saunders* in Works Grey, c.1894. This was the first locomotive that Sir William Stanier worked on as a young apprentice. (GW Trust)

No. 14 *Charles Saunders* at Westbourne Park depot, London, rebuilt in 1894 from 2-4-0 'simple' locomotive. (Bob Miller/MLS Collection)

No.16 *Brunel*, as rebuilt in 1894 from 2-4-0 'simple', c.1900.
(Bob Miller/MLS Collection)

No.16 *Brunel* as rebuilt in 1894 and before receiving a Churchward parallel boiler with Belpaire firebox in 1901.
(GW Trust)

Dean converted 3000-3029 2-2-2s to 4-2-2s and built the capable 'Dean Singles' as they were known, that brought GW performance over the level routes of London-Bristol-Exeter to a new high, as fast and free-running as the four 'Armstrongs' were sluggish.

Attempts were made to overcome the problems of the 'Armstrongs,' involving lining up the diameter of the cylinders and reboilering. No.16 received a parallel boiler with a Belpaire firebox in 1901 and eventually all four received taper boilers and became identical with the other outside-framed 6ft 8in 4-4-0s (see chapter 2, page 31).

Dean 'single' 4-2-2 3031 *Achilles* posing in Works grey livery. (Bob Miller/MLS Collection)

A handsome Dean 'single' 4-2-2, 3023 *Swallow*, at Old Oak Common, a new Churchward large 31XX 2-6-2T behind, c.1910. (Bob Miller/MLS Collection)

No.14 *Charles Saunders* rebuilt from broad gauge 'simple' 2-4-0, at Bath with what is believed to be the 10.45am Paddington-Newport, c.1900. (MLS Collection)

OPERATION

During the 1890s, after initial rebuilding, the Armstrongs were worked mainly on the level route between London and Bristol, although one regular turn was the 10.45am Paddington-South Wales via Bath, Bristol Stapleton Road and the Severn Tunnel, as far as Newport, where they would change engines to a 'Duke' or 'Bulldog'. The train was allowed two hours to the Bath stop, 106.9 miles, and despite this relatively easy timing, the Armstrongs struggled to maintain time, especially if there were any p-way slacks en route. The return diagram was the 6.40pm Paddington arrival from Newport allowed a full two hours and fifteen minutes non-stop from Bath. A return trip in the first decade of the twentieth century

TABLE 1 – 10.45 Paddington-Bath				
No.14 *Charles Saunders* 7 vehicles, 150 tons				
Distance Miles	Location	Actual mins secs	Average speed mph	Estimated top speeds mph
0.0	Paddington	00.00	-	
	Southall	-	-	pws 40*
18.5	Slough	25.10	44.0	52
36.0	Reading	44.58	53.3	56
53.1	Didcot	63.48	54.4	58
77.3	Swindon	92.28	50.7	speed trailing off to 46
	Hay Lane	-	-	pws 40*
	Dauntsey	-	-	67
94.0	Chippenham	112.26	50.0	
106.9	**Bath**	**127.46**	50.7	60

timed by Charles Rous-Marten and recorded in the *Railway Magazine* recounts a mediocre performance behind No.14 *Charles Saunders* on a load of 150 tons in the down direction and 170 tons in the up.

With two p-way slacks at Southall and Hay Lane costing three minutes

according to Rous-Marten, No.14 lost nearly eight minutes to the Bath stop. He recorded the following times shown above (Table 1).

It was found that the large cylinders often beat the boiler and there is evidence on this journey that steam pressure had dropped on the steady slightly rising gradients between Didcot and Swindon. Later, presumably as a result of this reputation, the cylinder diameter was reduced and in the post 1915 rebuildings, it was reduced a second time, at the same time as a Churchward boiler was provided. Compared with the later Badmintons and the Dean 'Singles', their poor performance cause is a matter of such conjecture – O.S. Nock suggested that a misjudgement in their port openings and steam passages might have led to a restriction in the flow of steam.

The return journey with an even easier schedule was not much better (Table 2).

Arrival at Paddington was just half a minute late, the net time being 129 minutes.

TABLE 2 – 4.25pm Bath-Paddington

No.14 *Charles Saunders*
8 vehicles, 170 tons

Distance Miles	Location	Actual mins secs	Average speed mph	Estimated top speeds mph
0.0	Bath	00.00		
	Box	-		pws 40*
12.9	Chippenham	21.01	36.8	45
-	Dauntsey	-		60/35
-	Hay Lane	-	-	pws 40*
29.6	Swindon	43.38	44.3	50/60
	Foxhall Junction	-	-	sig stand (momentary)
53.8	Didcot	73.54	50.0	
70.9	Reading	94.33	49.5	55
88.4	Slough	113.34	55.2	60
	Southall	-	-	58
106.9	**Paddington**	**135.28**	50.7	

One of the 'Armstrong' 4-4-0s, No. 8 *Gooch*, still unrebuilt, at speed on Goring troughs with the 10.45 Paddington-Cardiff via Bath and Bristol Stapleton Road, c.1902. (GW Trust)

Former Dean 'simple' 2-4-0 No.16, rebuilt in 1894 as a 4-4-0 and named *Brunel*, and fitted with parallel boiler and Belpaire firebox in 1901, seen here on Goring troughs with an up express, c.1909. (Bob Miller/MLS Collection)

Dean 'Single' 4-2-2 3069 *Earl of Chester* at speed with a Bristol-Paddington express near Hayes, c.1905.
(Bob Miller/MLS Collection)

Two Dean 'Singles' double-head an up express at Acton, the line from Acton Yard to the North London line in the background. In the first decade of the twentieth century, train loads were becoming heavy requiring double-heading and leading to the adoption of the 4-4-0 wheel arrangement on the GWR.
(Bob Miller/MLS Collection)

No.16 *Brunel* (later 4169) was recorded in 1909 on the 2.15pm Paddington-Birmingham via Oxford, a few months before the Bicester direct route was opened, and just before it received a Standard No.2 taper boiler – at this time it had the 1901 straight domeless boiler similar to the parallel Belpaire boilered 'Badmintons' (as seen in the photo on page 23). Overleaf is the log, a typical performance of this engine at this time (Table 3).

This was not a bad effort – a brisk start and respectable time to Oxford,

TABLE 3 – 2.15pm Paddington-Birmingham via Oxford, 1909

16 *Brunel*
7 coaches, 190 tons to Banbury (1 vehicle slipped)
6 coaches, 165 tons to Leamington (1 vehicle slipped)
5 coaches, 130 tons to Birmingham

Distance Miles	Location	Actual mins secs	Speed mph	Schedule
0.0	Paddington	00.00		T
1.3	Westbourne Park	02.56		
5.7	Ealing Broadway	08.28		
9.1	Southall	12.00	58	
13.2	West Drayton	16.03	61	
18.5	Slough	20.50	64	
24.2	Maidenhead	26.12	62	
31.0	Twyford	32.36	63½	
36.0	Reading	37.45	sigs 35*	
44.8	Goring	47.23	63	
48.5	Cholsey	50.55	65	
52.8	Didcot East Jcn	54.56	52*	
58.3	Radley	60.25	60	
63.4	Oxford	65.24	61½	
69.0	Kidlington	71.26	57	
75.1	Heyford	78.05	59	
80.2	Aynho Jcn	83.32	58	
86.1	Banbury	89.46	sigs 10*	1¼ E
89.7	Cropredy	94.30	51	
94.8	Fenny Compton	102.07	59	
99.8	Southam Road	106.57	65	
105.9	Leamington	113.30	40*	½ L
107.9	Warwick	115.50	56	
112.1	Hatton	120.37	47	
116.3	Lapworth	125.03	60	
118.8	Knowle	127.40	61	
122.2	Solihull	131.12	61	
128.8	Bordesley	139.05	p-way slack 15*	
129.3	**Birmingham**	**141.12**	**(135½ net)**	1¼ L

a bit sluggish on to Banbury and Leamington (65mph maximum before Leamington was sub-standard) but then a good climb to Hatton, although after two slip coaches had been detached the load was only 130 tons. However, with the planned pws before Bordesley, it had too little in hand to achieve a precise on time arrival. Despite the number of other double-framed 4-4-0s about then, most with taper boilers, it was surprising that a non-stop Birmingham service was entrusted to a parallel-boilered 'Armstrong'.

In contrast the Dean 4-2-2s were speedy engines and had the

Dean 'Single' 3019 *Rover* at an unknown location.
(Bob Miller/MLS Collection)

Dean 'Single' 3031 *Achilles* at Old Oak Common West with a down express, c.1900.
(Bob Miller/MLS Collection)

3060, a Dean 'Single' on an up Birmingham-London express passing Bordesley, c.1905.
(Bob Miller/MLS Collection)

monopoly of fast trains on the Paddington-Bristol-Exeter route until sufficient 'Badmintons' and 'Atbaras' came onto the scene. Rous-Marten recorded speeds of up to 83.3mph behind these engines, and the *Railway Magazine* of June 1901 published a run from Paddington to the outskirts of Birmingham at Bordesley covering the 128¼ miles in 142minutes 20 seconds at an average speed of 56mph , with a speed in excess of 70mph at Fosse Road (otherwise almost identical to No.16 above, but with double the load – 10 coaches). The locomotive was 3051 *Stormy Petrel*.

CHAPTER 2

CHURCHWARD'S INFLUENCE

Churchward was appointed as Dean's assistant in 1897 and had the very delicate task of supporting him during his final years in theoretical charge, as Dean's mental health deteriorated. Churchward conducted this difficult role with great sympathy and sensitivity and many of the late developments of both the small and large wheeled 4-4-0s at the end of the century owed much to Churchward building on Dean's basic earlier designs. Dean eventually retired in 1902, aged sixty-three; he died in 1905 aged sixty-six.

Churchward, his successor and virtual co-manager during the final five years or so, was born in 1857 in Stoke Gabriel on the River Dart between Kingswear and Totnes and joined the South Devon Railway at Newton Abbot in 1873. After absorption of that railway by the Great Western in 1876, he transferred, aged just nineteen to the Swindon Drawing Office, and after a few rapid promotions, was appointed as Carriage and Wagon Works Manager in 1885. Ten years later he became Swindon Works

Manager and identified as Dean's successor when he became his Chief Assistant in 1897, at a salary of £900 a year. Although he was not appointed as Locomotive Superintendent until 1 June 1902 – with his salary increased to £2,500 – he had been developing his ideas within the ample scope given him by Dean, and had already written a paper on a scheme for a limited number of 'standard' locomotive designs by January 1901, although in the interim he maintained a steady production of Dean designed engines, albeit showing an increasing influence of his own ideas, especially boiler design.

The 1901 paper outlined a scheme for six standard locomotive classes, a 2-8-0, two 4-6-0s, a 4-4-0, a 2-6-2 tank, and a 4-4-2 tank. The first 4-6-0, No.98 (later 2900), was built within a month of Churchward's formal appointment and the 2-8-0, No.97 (later 2800), was the second standard locomotive to emerge from Swindon Works in June 1903. By 1905, he had amassed sufficient experience of these prototypes to proceed with confidence and the standard 4-6-0s, 2-8-0s and 2-6-2 tanks began to be

built in quantity. Only then did the building of double-framed passenger 4-4-0s cease. Churchward finalised his plans for the full range of standard locomotives to meet all the Great Western Railway's needs, which, as well as the passenger locomotives, included the 2-6-0 mixed traffic 4300, which would cover the traffic needs that the small-wheeled 4-4-0s were still meeting. Its introduction in 1911 eliminated the need to build further 'Bulldog' small-wheeled 4-4-0s.

George Jackson Churchward, 1857-1933, Locomotive Superintendent (1902-1916) and Chief Mechanical Engineer (1916-1922) of the Great Western Railway.
(GW official photograph/NRM Collection)

3295 *Bessborough* with GW BR4 boiler and Belpaire firebox.
(MLS Collection)

BOILER DEVELOPMENTS

While he was developing his ideas for the GW's standard fleet of locomotives, he was using his time when he was nominally assisting Dean, experimenting with locomotive design concepts in both France and the USA that interested him. In particular, he was drawn to boiler design, firstly adopting the Belgian raised Belpaire firebox, then developing domeless boilers, building prototypes on both 5ft 8in and 6ft 8in 4-4-0 designs, that led to coned boilers, then taper boilers standardised as Swindon No.2 and Swindon No.4 which came to be fitted to numerous GW classes over the following half century.

In the descriptions of the 'Badmintons', 'Atbaras', 'Flowers' and 'Cities' to follow there will be numerous references to different types of boilers that Churchward designed in the period between 1897 and his assumption of full control in 1902. It is perhaps therefore best to describe and illustrate them at this point.

The 6ft 8in 'Badmintons' were introduced in December 1897, and these had the GW BR4 boilers – the conventional Dean boiler but with raised Belpaire firebox, illustrated in the photo of 3295 *Bessborough* above.

The 5ft 8in 4-4-0 3312 *Bulldog* was fitted with a larger domed boiler, the precursor of the Swindon No.2 standard boiler, and a similar domeless version was fitted in January 1899 to the nineteenth 'Badminton' to be constructed, 3310 *Waterford*, illustrated on the next page.

Churchward then fitted the BR4 boiler with raised Belpaire firebox to the last four 'Dukes', 3328-3331 built in July/August 1899, whilst developing even larger and heavier boilers for his 4-4-0s and 4-6-0s. He also allowed his assistant, F.G.

3310 *Waterford* as built with BR0 boiler that became Swindon Standard No.2. (J.M. Bentley)

3297 *Earl Cawdor* with the S4X boiler designed by F.G. Wright, 1903. (MLS Collection)

Wright, to experiment with an even larger boiler, the S4X round-topped with increased heating surface, dome and drumhead smokebox, which engine 3297 *Earl Cawdor* carried from July 1903 until 1906.

Churchward enlarged the prototype No.2 boiler increasing pressure to 200lb and the heating surface to 1,818.12sqft, initially on an 'Atbara' (3405), then to the 1903 'Cities' and to all but three of the 'Badmintons' as seen on the next page on 3305 *Samson*.

Finally, many of the 4-4-0s developed frame problems under the heavy No.4 boiler and the earlier engines, including all the 'Badmintons' were re-equipped with the lighter Swindon Standard No.2 taper boilers, superheated after 1911.

3305 *Samson* fitted with an un-superheated Swindon Standard No.4 boiler in November 1905, seen here at Weymouth, c.1910. (J.M. Bentley/Photomatic)

4103 *Bessborough* with superheated Standard No.2 boiler, seen here shortly before its withdrawal in April 1930. (J M Bentley Collection)

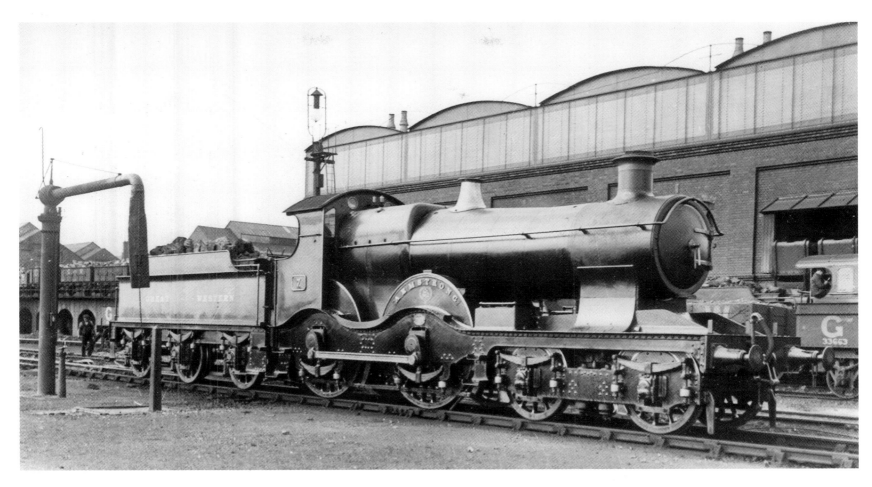

REBUILDING THE 'ARMSTRONGS'

As well as developing the new boilers for the later Dean and his own 4-4-0s, Churchward decided to do something about the unsatisfactory performance of the four 'Armstrong' 4-4-0s. At first, he rebuilt No.16 *Brunel* in 1901 with a large domeless boiler with raised Belpaire firebox. It received a Standard No.2 boiler in 1909, pressed at 180lb and increasing the tractive effort to over 18,000lb. No.7 was rebuilt in 1905 with the Swindon No.2 boiler and cast iron chimney and changed boilers in 1909 receiving one with a copper capped chimney. No.14 also received a No.2 boiler with copper capped chimney in 1909. No.8 was rebuilt in 1911 with a superheated short-cone boiler. The other three locomotives were superheated between 1911 and 1913. The new boilers increased the weight of the engines to 54 tons 14 cwt, 91 tons 9 cwt including tender, and the axle-weight to 18½ tons.

Further rebuilding took place from 1915, when the locomotives were brought into line with the 'Flower' class, the driving wheel diameter being reduced to 6ft 8½ in, the bogie wheel diameter from 4ft 1in to the standard 3ft 8in and the cylinders lined up to 18in x 26in. They were renumbered in the order of rebuilding immediately after the 'Flowers' and rather than applying

No.7 *Armstrong* as rebuilt with Swindon No.2 standard boiler in 1909 but before rebuilding as a 'Flower' class with 6ft 8½in coupled wheels in 1923, seen here at Wolverhampton Stafford Road, c.1912. (GW Trust)

No.14 *Charles Saunders* rebuilt with the No.2 taper boiler, but before rebuilding as a 'Flower' class in 1917, c.1910.
(GW Trust)

No.14 *Charles Saunders* at Swindon with No.2 boiler as rebuilt in 1909, here before rebuilding as a 'Flower' class in 1917.
(GW Trust)

their previous numerical order, No.16, rebuilt first in April 1915, became 4169, No.14 which was rebuilt in May 1917 became 4170, and the final two were not rebuilt until February 1923, No.7 becoming 4171 and No.8, 4172. With the heavier boilers, their axle-weight increased to 18½ tons. Interestingly, their frames never needed strengthening unlike many of the other double-framed 4-4-0s. They were not fitted with ATC, being withdrawn between 1928 and 1930. Over their career as 4-4-0s, all four had amassed over a million miles in traffic.

After the 1909 reboilerings, the four locomotives were reallocated to the Wolverhampton Division and spent the rest of their lives working on the Northern Road via Oxford and Bicester and also north of Wolverhampton, though there appears to be no record of any logs of them either after reboilering or the rebuilding identical to the 'Flower' class. As they were not prematurely scrapped but remained until 1928-30, about the same as the other GW 6ft 8in double-framed 4-4-0s, it can be assumed that their performance was sufficiently improved and comparable with the other 4-4-0s although by the time of their rebuilding they would have had few opportunities for demanding work.

No.16 *Brunel* as rebuilt in 1901 with parallel boiler and Belpaire firebox, c.1905. (GW Trust)

No.14 *Charles Saunders*, rebuilt in 1909 with Swindon Standard No.2 boiler and copper-cap chimney, on arrival at Oxford from Paddington, c.1910.
(A.G. Ellis/M.L. Boakes Collection)

No.16 *Brunel* rebuilt in 1909 with No.2 standard boiler at Bentley Heath with a Birmingham-Bournemouth train composed of LSWR rolling stock, c.1911. (GW Trust)

No.16 *Brunel* rebuilt as 4169 in 1915 with 6ft 8½ in diameter coupled wheels and 18in x 26in cylinders as a 'Flower' class, seen here in the 1920s. (Bob Miller/MLS Collection)

4171 *Armstrong* rebuilt in 1909 with No.2 standard boiler and in 1923 with 6ft 8½ in coupled wheels, seen here shortly before withdrawal in the late 1920s. (Bob Miller/MLS Collection)

Dean rebuilt 4-4-0 No.8 *Gooch*, reboilered by Churchward in 1911 and rebuilt as a 6ft 8½in 'Flower' in 1923 and renumbered 4172.
(Bob Miller/MLS Collection)

4171 *Armstrong* in final condition as rebuilt in 1923, seen here near the end of its life on a freight at Chester c.1927.
(GW Trust)

Swindon Dump with a number of withdrawn locomotives awaiting scrapping, including 4172 *Brunel*, 'Flower' 4163 *Marigold*, 'City' 3707 *Malta* and a number of ROD 2-8-0s, May 1929 (GW Trust)

4172 *Gooch* in final form after rebuilding as a 'Flower' class in 1923, seen here on a Cardiff-Bristol-Salisbury train at Warminster, 29 April 1928. (GW Trust)

CHAPTER 3

THE 'BADMINTONS'

DESIGN & CONSTRUCTION

The new 'Badminton', 3292, before naming, built with BR4 boiler and raised Belpaire firebox and with the original design of cab with side window, January 1898. (Bob Miller/MLS Collection)

During the period when Churchward took an increasing role in the design and management of GWR locomotive matters he was taking an interest in locomotive design and practice in the USA, particularly in the development of large higher pressure boilers. With the discreet approval of the GW Board, Churchward began to plan for the modernisation and standardisation of the GW's locomotive fleet, but in the interim period he began to incorporate some of his own ideas in designs that were still at least nominally Dean's.

Despite the success of the Dean 'Singles' east of Exeter, it was becoming apparent that passenger loads were increasing and the success of Dean's 5ft 8in 'Dukes' in Devon and Cornwall led to the building of a large wheeled 6ft 8in version of the Dukes. 3292 was completed and emerged from Swindon Works in December 1897, seeming on outward glance to be a 6ft 8in version of the 'Dukes' and similar in some ways to the 'Armstrongs', although it had smaller cylinders – 18in diameter x 26in stroke – and higher boiler pressure of 180lb. Under the obvious influence of Churchward, and late in the design stage, 3292 was equipped with a Belpaire firebox, which Churchward was to fit to the last four 'Dukes' a year or so later. The appearance of the new locomotive startled enthusiasts of the day who considered the 'Badmintons', as they became known, as ugly as the 'Armstrongs' were handsome. The grate area, 18.32sqft and heating surface, 1,296.9sqft, were smaller than those of the 'Armstrongs', but the Belpaire firebox allowed greater steam space above the boiler water line.

Another visual change was the design of the cab, which included both large forward–looking spectacles and a side square window

high up in the cab sides. 3292 was unnamed initially and only received its name, *Badminton*, four months later, at the same time as the building of the second locomotive, *Barrington*. In fact, for a short while these 4-4-0s were identified as the 'Barrington' class. Further dimensions of the new engines were bogie wheels of 4ft diameter, axle-weight over the coupled wheels of 17 tons 1 cwt, engine weight of 52 tons 2 cwt, with tender, 84 tons 13 cwt. Tractive effort at 85% was 16,010 lb. After the four-month gap, Swindon was given the go-ahead and built a further eleven in three months, at one stage turning out a new locomotive every week. 3292 was named in April 1898 and the other locomotives of the class were numbered and named as follows:

3293 *Barrington*
3294 *Blenheim*
3295 *Bessborough*
3296 *Cambria*
3297 *Earl Cawdor*
3298 *Grosvenor*
3299 *Hubbard*
3300 *Hotspur*
3301 *Monarch*
3302 *Mortimer*
3303 *Marlborough*

Earl Cawdor was the name of the Chairman of the GWR at the time and several of the other names were directors of the company, with 3299 and 3302 having their Christian names, Alexander and Charles respectively, added subsequently.

After a gap of a couple of months, eight further 'Badmintons' were built between September 1898

and January 1899, bearing the following names and numbers:

3304 *Oxford*
3305 *Samson*
3306 *Shelburne*
3307 *Shrewsbury*
3308 *Savernake*
3309 *Shakespeare*
3310 *Waterford*
3311 *Wynnstay*

All these locomotives were built to the same design except for the penultimate one, 3310, which appeared with a prototype of the Swindon No.2 boiler, similar to one fitted to the 'Bulldog' 3312 in October 1898, except that 3310's was domeless. 3310 was constructed in January 1899 and Churchward had four raised Belpaire boilers fitted to

3292 Badminton at Swindon, after naming and modifications to the cab, c.1905.
(Bob Miller/MLS Collection)

The first named 'Badminton', 3293 Barrington, built in April 1898, at Westbourne Park, Paddington, c.1898.
(J.M. Bentley Collection)

3295 *Bessborough*, built in May 1898, shortly after delivery that year, and with frames, splashers, cab and tender subject to 'guivering' with tallow by the cleaners – usually at the instruction of the driver.
(J.M. Bentley Collection)

3297 *Earl Cawdor* in original condition with BR4 boiler before rebuilding in 1903 with F G Wright's designed larger boiler, seen here at Swindon prior to working a royal train, c.1902.
(J.M. Bentley Collection)

3300 *Hotspur* as built in July 1898.
(Bob Miller/MLS Collection)

3302 *Mortimer*, (later renamed *Charles Mortimer*) one of four 'Badmintons' built in July 1898.
(J.M. Bentley Collection)

3304 *Oxford*, the first engine of the second batch, built in September 1898. (J.M. Bentley Collection)

3308 *Savernake* as built in 1898, seen here at Weymouth c.1905. (GW Trust)

3309 *Shakespeare* at an unknown location, before rebuilding with a No.2 standard boiler, c.1905.
(J.M. Bentley Collection)

3311 *Wynnstay*, the last of the twenty 'Badminton' class, as built in January 1899, c.1903.
(J.M. Bentley Collection)

3310 *Waterford*, as built with the Churchward prototype domeless boiler and unique cab design in 1899.
(J.M. Bentley Collection)

3310 *Waterford*, as originally built and in service c.1900.
(Bob Miller/MLS Collection)

the last four 'Dukes' in July-August 1899. 3310 had a steel firebox and Ramsbottom type safety valves and a larger cab with combined number and name on the cabside. Its dimensions varied from the standard

'Badminton' class as, in addition, its total heating surface was increased to 1,520.3sqft; the grate area also was larger at 23.65sqft, and the total engine weight was 52 tons 10 cwt. The boiler was also erected at a

higher pitch. This boiler was further developed as the Swindon Standard No.2 coned boiler and was fitted to the first production run of 'Bulldogs' in October 1899. 3310 went through a further change in November 1903 when its experimental boiler was replaced by a Swindon No.4 boiler as fitted to the 'Cities', although it retained its non-standard cab.

In 1903, 3297 *Earl Cawdor* was selected for a further boiler experiment. Churchward's assistant, F.G. Wright, persuaded Churchward to fit this engine with a very large flush round top boiler with high water reservoir capacity. It had a significantly larger heating surface at 1,934.02sqft, a smaller grate area of 17.85sqft, but a higher boiler pressure of 210lb. It was thought that the greater hot water reservoir space would give the locomotive assistance on routes with undulating gradients and in many ways the boiler was similar to that of the Bowen-Cooke 'Precursor' 4-4-0s on the LNWR, with a deep firebox and horizontal grate – although in fact, 3297 preceded the 'Precursors' by several months. It was also equipped with a large double-side window cab of the North Eastern or Great Eastern pattern. The engine weight was 56 tons 14 cwt and its axle-weight went up to 19 tons. The NE style cab was replaced by a standard GW one in November 1904 and the boiler, which showed no improvement over the Churchward boiler but was much heavier, was replaced in 1906. Experience with the LNWR boilers suggested that the engines went best with a fairly thick fire – which may have put the engine

3310 *Waterford*, as rebuilt with an un-superheated Swindon No. 4 ('City') boiler in November 1903. (Bob Miller/MLS Collection)

at some disadvantage with GW crews used to different firing methods.

All but three of the Badmintons (3301, 3302 and 3304) were rebuilt with Standard No.4 ('City') boilers between 1905 and 1910, making them in effect equivalent to the 'City' class, and similar to 3310 *Waterford* which had been reboilered in 1903. The heating surface was increased to 1,818.12sqft, the grate area to 20.56sqft, and boiler pressure to 200lbpsi. The axle-weight over the coupled wheels increased to 18 tons and the total weight of the engine was 56 tons. Initially they had cast iron chimneys but from 1907 most carried chimneys with copper caps.

These boilers were carried until 1911-13, but frame problems began to occur under the heavy boiler and

3297 *Earl Cawdor* as rebuilt at Swindon by Churchward's assistant, F.G. Wright, with large flush round topped boiler and NE style cab in 1903 seen here a year later and before receiving a standard GW cab in 1904 and boiler in 1906. (J.M. Bentley/Photomatic)

3297 *Earl Cawdor* at Oxford in 1904 rebuilt with GW style cab but retaining its large diameter boiler, exchanged a couple of years later for a GW Swindon Standard No.2. (MLS Collection)

3298 *Grosvenor*, rebuilt with Swindon large No.4 standard boiler, at Paddington awaiting departure with a down express, c.1906. (GW Trust)

all twenty locomotives were finally fitted with smaller Standard No.2 boilers, about 3½ tons lighter, although strengthened frames retained the overall engine weight at around 56 tons. The weight varied from engine to engine, ranging from 52½ tons to 56 with an average of 54, and axle-weight of 17 tons 10 cwt. Some locomotives were superheated when they still had the No.4 boiler and all the No.2 boilers received superheating between 1912 and the end of 1916. Top feed was fitted from 1911.

All were renumbered in 1912, using the numbers 4100-4119. 4112 *Oxford* and 4115 *Shrewsbury* lost their

3298 *Grosvenor*, fitted in 1905 with a Standard No.4 boiler and with a cast iron chimney (replaced by copper-capped chimney in 1907) with a down express at Paddington station, c.1906. (J.M. Bentley Collection)

3294 *Blenheim* as fitted with a Swindon No.4 standard boiler, c.1906. (GW Trust)

3299 *Alexander Hubbard*, rebuilt with a No.4 boiler in December 1905, here at Gloucester, 3 April 1906. (J.M. Bentley Collection)

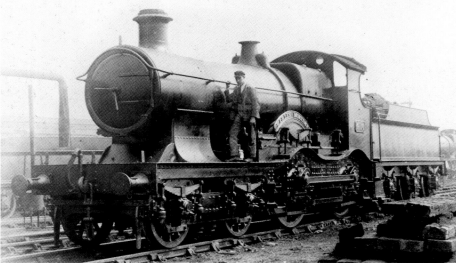

4110 *Charles Mortimer* at Swindon after fitting with a No.2 boiler and copper cap chimney in March 1911, seen here after renumbering, c.1913. 4110 was one of three 'Badmintons' that never received a No.4 boiler, but went straight from the Dean BR4 to the Swindon No.2.
(A.G. Ellis/J.M. Bentley Collection)

names in 1927, when the company decided that engines having place names on its routes caused confusion to passengers, some of whom might think the engine was showing the train's destination. None of the engines received ATC equipment, as they were all withdrawn from traffic like most of the other large-wheeled 4-4-0s between 1927 and 1931. The last survivors were 4109 *Monarch* and 4115, withdrawn in March 1931 from Bristol Bath Road and Tyseley respectively and 4113 *Samson* of Didcot which lasted just two months more to May 1931.

The prototype 4100 *Badminton* with superheated No.2 boiler at Exeter in 1926.
(SLS/J.M. Bentley Collection)

4110 *Charles Mortimer* (originally named just *Mortimer*) at Worcester, April 1923.
(A.G. Ellis/J.M. Bentley Collection)

4101 *Barrington* on shed in the 1920s.
(J.M. Bentley/Real Photographs)

4108 *Hotspur* with No.2 boiler and cast iron chimney at Bristol Bath Road depot, September 1927.
(SLS/J.M. Bentley Collection)

4108 *Hotspur* from the other side at Bath Road depot, September 1927.
(SLS/J.M. Bentley Collection)

Unnamed 4115 at Shrewsbury station (where its previous name may have caused some confusion) with a North & West express for Hereford and Pontypool Road, c.1928. (J.M. Bentley Collection/Photomatic)

4115 *Shrewsbury* at Reading on an up semi-fast from Oxford to Paddington, before its name was removed to avoid passenger confusion in 1927.
(J.M. Bentley Collection)

4115 after removal of name (*Shrewsbury*) at Tyseley, 3 July 1929.
(J.M. Bentley Collection)

The unique 3310 *Waterford*, renumbered 4118, seen here at the end of its life at Swindon dump, July 1927. Its prototype No.2 boiler was replaced by a No.4 boiler in 1903 and a No.2 superheated boiler, as seen in this photo, in March 1912. (J.M. Bentley Collection)

4113 *Samson*, the last 'Badminton survivor, seen here in front of a 45XX 2-6-2T at Swindon during its last overhaul, c.1929.
(J.M. Bentley Collection/Real Photographs)

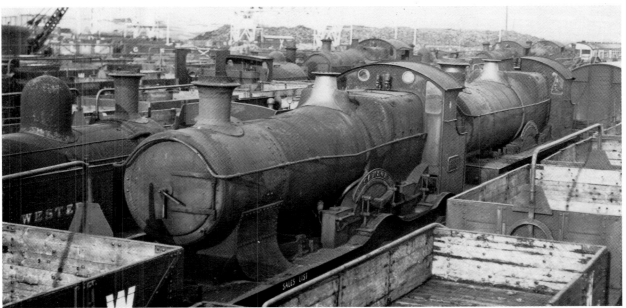

4113 *Samson* two years after its withdrawal in May 1931, with Churchward 'County' 3805 *County Kerry*, in a row of locomotives awaiting scrapping on the Swindon dump, 29 October 1933.
(H.C. Casserley/J.M. Bentley Collection)

3303 *Marlborough* with a North & West express Church Stretton c.1900.
(J.M. Bentley Collection)

TABLE 4
2.50pm Shrewsbury-Bristol Wool Buyers' Special

3301 *Monarch*
5chs, 127/135 tons gross

Distance Miles	Location	Actual mins secs	Speed mph
0.0	Shrewsbury	00.00	Priming
4.2	Condover	08.39	35
6.4	Dorrington	11.16	53
9.3	Leebotwood	15.08	40½ /pws 35*
12.8	Church Stretton	20.37	38/35
19.9	Craven Arms	27.15	77/75
22.9	Onibury	29.30	77/72
27.5	Ludlow	33.29	62*
32.1	Woofferton	37.31	72/61
38.4	Leominster	43.17	69/65
44.0	MP 44	48.36	60
46.8	Moreton-on-Lugg	51.07	68/60
51.0	**Hereford**	**55.47**	
3.0	Rotherwas	07.15	40
10.0	Tram Inn	14.42	68
15.0	Pontrilas	19.22	60
19.0	Llanvihangel	24.35	43½
24.0	Abergavenny	30.13	pws 10*/58
29.0	Nantyderry	35.25	pws 4*
34.0	Pontypool Road	43.25	65/25*
	Maindee Jcn W	50.40	pws 10*
	Severn Tunnel Jcn	60.50	pws in tunnel
	Patchway	-	44½
68.4	**Bristol T M**	**83.05**	

OPERATION

Initially, the new 'Badmintons' were allocated to the Westbourne Park and Bristol Bath Road depots to relieve the Dean 4-2-2 'Singles' that were still on top of their work, provided the load was not too great. Then, as train loads increased further, the new 'Saints' and 'Stars' came along, and the 'Badmintons' were displaced from the main West of England work and were found more frequently on the Bristol-Shrewsbury 'North & West' route and on the Paddington-Wolverhampton via Oxford line. They also took over South Wales expresses from the '3232' class of 2-4-0s until in later years the 'Saints' relieved the 4-4-0s.

In 1899, the GW ran with the LNWR a 'wool buyers' special from Bradford to Bristol Docks (in competition with the Midland route)

which reached speeds between Shrewsbury and Bristol in both directions that were not reached again until diesel traction regularly ran the route from the summer of 1963. A.G. Robbins was on the footplate of 3301 *Monarch* in both directions (Table 4).

There were four slacks for track relaying between Hereford and Bristol and little opportunity for further fast running but climbing to Llanvihangel and out of the Severn Tunnel was swift. Robbins only recorded milepost timings between Hereford and Maindee Junction. Arrival was one minute before schedule. The full log for the return journey is given on the next page (Table 5).

Arrival at Shrewsbury was 3½ minutes early. Speeds assessed from average point to point times.

Later, Charles Rous-Marten published a log in the *Railway Magazine* of a return trip he made behind a 'Badminton' on the

TABLE 5
4.30pm Bristol Temple Meads-Shrewsbury Wool Buyers' Special

3301 *Monarch*
5chs, 127/135 tons gross

Distance Miles	Location	Actual mins secs	Speed mph
0.0	Bristol TM	00.00	
4.0	(Filton Bank)	07.30	39/33½
10.0	-	13.40	68
	Patchway	-	pws 40*
	Pilning	-	pws 10*
16.5	Severn Tnl Jcn	23.20	
25.7	Maindee W.Jcn	33.20	60/25*
30.2	(Caerleon MP 37)	39.05	54
34.2	(Llantarnam Jcn)	44.40	38½
34.8	Pontypool Rd	45.40	pws 5*
41.8	Penpergwm	52.45	72
44.5	Abergavenny	55.20	57
48.5	Llanvihangel	60.45	41
56.0	Pontrilas	67.10	82
59.2	(Tram Inn)	70.04	67
62.2	(Rotherwas)	72.42	67
65.1	Red Hill Jcn	75.15	70/35*
68.4	**Hereford**	**78.55**	
0.0		00.00	
1.0	(Barrs Court Jcn)	02.12	
7.5	Dinmore	09.30	60/pws 5*
10.2	Ford Bridge	12.45	35
12.6	Leominster	16.25	52
15.7	Berrington	20.05	60
18.9	Woofferton	23.03	65/75
23.5	Ludlow	27.20	56*
28.1	Onibury	31.40	52/69
31.1	Craven Arms	34.40	60
35.6	Marsh Brook	39.35	55
38.2	Church Stretton	42.47	48
41.7	Leebotwood	45.55	67
44.6	Dorrington	48.20	72
46.7	Condover	50.05	72
51.0	**Shrewsbury**	**55.45**	

3306 *Shelburne* with a northbound North & West express tops the summit at Church Stretton station, c.1900. (J.M. Bentley Collection)

Cornishman between Paddington and Exeter which similarly demonstrated what the new engines were capable of. The runs were made in the late Autumn of 1899 and published early the following year. The locomotive was 3298 *Grosvenor* and the load 8 vehicles, 220 tons gross. Departure from Paddington was 2 ½ minutes late which had been recovered in the first thirty miles. The 46 miles from Bristol to Taunton were covered in 47 minutes 44 seconds with speeds in the mid-60s for most of the way and the eleven miles from Taunton to Whiteball summit were covered in 14 minutes 47 seconds with 30mph at the top of the bank. Driver Millard brought his train into Exeter after descent in the low 70s a good 5½ minutes early, where 3298 gave way to a 'Duke'. The return journey, the 10.30am Plymouth, was booked non-stop from Exeter to Paddington, 193.7 miles, schedule 3 hours 45 minutes. The seven coach train was brought in from Plymouth by 'Duke' 3318 *Jupiter*.

I am comparing this with a run timed by W J Scott, in which he gave outline times of a run on the 3.50pm from Exeter, also non-stop on the same schedule, but with an extra coach, and encountering a strong side wind after Uphill Junction. The driver also complained that 3298 was high mileage and due for overhaul and was not steaming particularly well on parts of the journey. Despite this, the recorder reported that the engine still seemed capable of making any speed required easily. The descent from Whiteball to Taunton was almost

TABLE 6 12.05pm Exeter-Paddington				3.50 pm Exeter-Paddington	
3298 *Grosvenor* 7 chs, 165 tons gross				3298 *Grosvenor* 8 chs, 185 tons	
Distance Miles	Location	Actual mins secs	Speed mph	Actual mins secs	Punctuality
0.0	Exeter	00.00		00.00	T
3.5	Stoke Canon	06.17	50		
7.2	Silverton	10.27	55		
8.4	Hele	11.53	50		
12.6	Collumpton	16.15	57/62	17.15	
14.8	Tiverton Jcn	18.59	52	20.00	1L
19.2	Burlescombe	24.18	49		
19.9	Whiteball Box	25.26	47	26.31	
23.7	Wellington	29.16	68/83½	30.19	
28.8	Norton F'warren	33.04	78		
30.8	Taunton	34.48	50*	35.53	1E
36.6	Durston	41.16	58		
42.3	Bridgwater	46.40	65		
44.9	Dunball	49.10	63 eased		
48.6	Highbridge	55.12	pws 25*		
55.3	Bleadon	62.06	60		
58.8	Worle Jcn	65.18	67		
63.6	Yatton	69.56	60		
67.5	Nailsea	73.44	63		
69.9	Flax Bourton	75.57	66		
74.5	Bedminster	80.26	60 eased		
75.2	Pylle Hill Jcn	81.56	25*	80.30	
77.9	Bristol East	86.26	35*	83.30	7½ E
80.1	Keynsham	89.59	50		
82.5	Saltford	92.45	55		
87.0	Bath	97.23	60/30*	96.15 sigs	6¾ E
89.3	Bathampton	100.48	45		
92.0	Box	103.56	55/45	102.40	
95.6	Corsham	108.46	50	108.15	
99.9	Chippenham	113.52	45/60	113.20	6¾ E
106.2	Dauntsey	119.24	75/50	119.32	
111.0	Wootton Bassett	124.56	55	125.40	
116.4	Swindon	130.59	55	132.10	7¾ E
122.1	Shrivenham	136.32	65		
127.2	Uffington	141.00	70		
129.8	Challow	143.18	68		
133.3	Wantage Road	146.12	75		
137.2	Steventon	149.29	72		
140.6	Didcot	152.16	75	155.03 sigs	11 E
	Cholsey	-	pws 45*		
152.2	Pangbourne	165.22	55		
155.1	Tilehurst	168.03	65 eased		
157.7	Reading	171.17	40*	171.45 pws*	13¼ E
162.7	Twyford	179.02	pws 40*		
169.5	Maidenhead	185.47	58		
171.3	Taplow	187.30	60		
175.2	Slough	191.09	65	193.12	9¾ E
180.5	West Drayton	196.10	65		
184.6	Southall	200.13	62	202.48	10¼ E
188.0	Ealing B'way	203.24	63	206.05	
189.5	Acton	204.52	60		
193.7	**Paddington**	**209.56**		**212.42**	**12¼ E**

3298 *Grosvenor* halts at Bath with a down express for Bristol and the West of England, c.1900. The engine has been 'guivered'.
(J.M. Bentley Collection/Real Photographs)

3300 *Hotspur* leaves Bristol with a train for Exeter and Plymouth, c.1900.
(J.M. Bentley Collection)

An unidentified 'Badminton' pauses at Dawlish station watched by an elderly gentleman in the town gardens, 1900. (J.M. Bentley Collection)

An unidentified 'Badminton' storms into action with a local passenger train at an unknown location, possibly Shrewsbury, c.1900. (J.M. Bentley Collection/P.W. Pilcher)

identical and a top speed in the low 80s is assumed and the Taunton-Bristol time was faster by about three minutes although unchecked. However, running so early, it clearly caught up a previous train at Bath and ran easily until Swindon, when normal speed was resumed.

The locomotive was eased after Reading to avoid too early an arrival, but it was still a full 15 minutes early at Paddington.

In an article of the *Railway Magazine* in 1900, entitled *Great Western Coupled Express Engines*, Charles Rous-Marten wrote:

Whether or not it was originally anticipated that the 'Badminton' engines would prove epoch-making in GW locomotive practice, I am

unable to say. Certainly they appear to have done so. And, curiously enough, their strong point is their remarkable fleetness. It cannot be said that they are beautiful to look at. They lack the graceful lines of the single-wheelers, but they assuredly have an unmistakeable look of sturdy power. A casual observer would say that they ought to pull anything, but that they do not look to have much speed about them. Yet it is their speed which is so noteworthy, especially with loads that would seriously hamper the single-wheelers. Testing

one of these 6ft 8in coupled engines down a falling gradient, I found it easily attained speeds of 78.2, 79.1, 80.3, 81.8, 82.5, 83.3, and finally 83.7 miles per hour. Even then the engine seemed to be running well within its powers and I do not doubt that a higher velocity could have been reached had this been advisable.

The *Railway Magazine* in the early 1900s published a number of other runs between London and Bath in the articles by Rous-Marten. 3292 *Badminton* on the 10.45 to South

Wales via Bristol (the train that the 'Armstrongs' had dominated for a number of years) reached the first stop, Bath, in two minutes under the two hours, a gain of seven minutes on the schedule, despite a severe p-way slowing at Foxhall Junction. It was through Slough in 22 minutes, 12 seconds, Reading in 39½ minutes and Didcot in 57¾ minutes before the slack. Speed on the level, hauling 178 tons was in the mid to high 60s. A run on the up return working with 3293 *Barrington* completed the 106.9 miles in 119 minutes 20 seconds with

3304 *Oxford* on a down express at Hayes, c.1900 – photo from which the Moore painting was copied.
(GW Trust)

3293 *Barrington* passes through Westbourne Park with a down Newbury Race special whilst Dean Goods No.2507 takes a set of empty coaches back to the carriage sidings, c.1898.
(Bob Miller/MLS Collection)

3302 *Charles Mortimer* departs Paddington and passes Subway Junction with a down express, c.1902. (GW Trust)

3303 *Charles Mortimer* with a Bristol-Paddington train near Saltford, c.1902. (GW Trust)

3293 *Barrington* at Wolverhampton Low Level ready to depart with a southbound train, c.1900.
(A.G. Ellis/J.M. Bentley Collection)

204 tons behind the tender, arriving some 15 minutes early on the easy schedule, with speed held steadily around the 60mph level for some seventy miles east of Swindon.

The 'Badmintons' also did sterling work on the northern road to Wolverhampton via both Oxford and later, via Bicester. J C Keyte had a log published by the *Railway Magazine* of a run from Leaminton to Paddington that he enjoyed in 1910, the first year the direct route via Bicester was opened. At the time the engine concerned, 3298 again (this engine seems to figure prominently in the best runs of the time) was fitted with a Standard No.4 'City' boiler, a year before reboilering with a superheated

3293 *Barrington* at Weymouth, c.1900.
(GW Trust)

3306 *Shelburne* double-heading a Dean 2-2-2 in the Wolverhampton area, c.1900.
(J.M. Bentley Collection)

Standard No.2. Note particularly the high speed on the last lap through Gerrard's Cross and Denham, (see Table 7 on page 67).

I have not found any records of the performance of the large-boilered 3297 during the three year period when it had the 'Wright' boiler. There is a record of a conversation with a driver when 3297 had arrived (on time) with Ocean Mails from Plymouth, but despite this the driver was clearly not impressed with the engine, saying that 'it needed coaxing' and was less free-running than other members of the class. Evidence of authority's opinion of the engine is perhaps illustrated by the fact that it was regularly rostered to a heavy train of siphons containing empty milk churns that

3297 *Earl Cawdor* with F G Wright's large diameter round-topped boiler (S4X type) with a down fast passenger train near Acton, 1903. (MLS Collection)

3297 *Earl Cawdor* moves westbound near Acton, with a Kensington (Addison Road)-Swindon train of siphons full of empty milk churns, c.1904. 3297 still has the large boiler which was replaced by a Swindon No.4 boiler in 1906 and the NE type cab with was replaced by a GW type in 1905. (J.M. Bentley Collection)

ran daily from Kensington (Addison Road) to Swindon.

Once they had received Standard No.2 boilers, they were in the same pool as the 'Atbaras' and 'Flowers' that had been similarly reboilered. In 1922, at the amalgamation of the 'Big Four' railways, the twenty 'Badmintons' were allocated thus:

Cardiff (4):	4104, 4110, 4114, 4116
Landore (2):	4100, 4115
Tyseley (2):	4106, 4107,
Worcester (2):	4101, 4109
Oxford (2):	4102, 4119
Bristol (2):	4103, 4108
W'hampton :	4111
Shrewsbury:	4113
Banbury:	4112
Weston-s-M:	4118
Taunton:	4105
Swindon:	4117

3306 *Shelburne*, now fitted with a Swindon Standard No.2 boiler departs Paddington with a down express, c.1907. Its cast iron chimney was replaced by a copper-capped version later that year.
(J.M. Bentley Collection)

3300 *Hotspur*, with a standard No.4 boiler, cuts off from an unidentified 'Atbara' which it has piloted to Whiteball summit on a Plymouth-Paddington express, c.1907. A locomotive that has assisted westbound services to Whiteball is in the siding behind the up service.
(J.M. Bentley Collection)

O.S. Nock, in the David & Charles 1978 book *Standard Gauge Great Western 4-4-0s, Part 2* quotes a number of runs recorded by E.L. Bell of 4-4-0s working fast London-Birmingham trains in the period immediately after the Bicester cut-off opening in 1910. Cecil J Allen, in his regular *Railway Magazine* articles on 'Locomotive Practice and Performance', concentrates on the work of the GW 4-6-0s, but the 4-4-0s seem to have shared some of the hardest duties just prior to the First World War. Most of the recorded 4-4-0 runs are with 'Flowers' (see Chapter 5) or the outside cylinder 'Counties' and I cannot find any record of 'Badmintons' other than the one shown below with 3298. However, Mr Nock has

found a wartime run with a 'Badminton' rebuilt with a super-heated Standard No.2 boiler, 4119 *Wynnstay* (pre 1912 numbering 3311). As it had a load of 310 tons, it was given a pilot in the shape of a 2-4-0 of the '481' class, No.587, between Pontypool Road and Hereford , but went forward from Hereford unaided. The details noted are relatively brief, (Table 8 page 68).

O.S. Nock commented that the run from Pontypool Road to Hereford was taken in a fairly leisurely fashion (although under schedule), but north of Hereford *Wynnstay* and her crew displayed some energy, averaging 58.7mph from Dinmore to Ludlow. The start out of Hereford was slow, but after Dinmore it became much livelier with speeds in the upper 60s before

3295 Bessborough, with Standard No.2 boiler and copper-cap chimney, on a down Paddington-Oxford-Birmingham train near Acton, c.1910.
(J.M. Bentley Collection)

TABLE 7
Leamington Spa-Paddington, 1910

3298 *Grosvenor*
190/195 tons

Distance Miles	Location	Actual mins secs	Speed mph	Punctuality
0.0	Leamington	00.00		T
6.1	Southam Road	09.23	45/pws 30*	
11.1	Fenny Compton	16.25	42/48	
16.2	Cropredy	22.16	60	
19.8	Banbury	25.31	67	2 L
24.9	Aynho Junction	30.04	68	1½ L
30.1	Ardley	35.32	55	
33.9	Bicester	38.44	72/77½	
43.2	Ashendon Junction	46.35	72	1½ L
47.2	Haddenham	50.34	64	
52.6	Princes Risborough	55.55	60½ /56	2 L
55.1	Saunderton summit	58.47	50	
60.8	High Wycombe	64.21	65/60	1¼ L
65.6	Beaconsfield	70.05	48/52	
69.9	Gerrards Cross	74.03	65/80	
	Denham	-	88½	
77.0	Northolt Junction	79.18	81	¼ L
82.7	Park Royal	83.55	75/sigs	
87.3	**Paddington**	**92.19**		**¼ L**

3293 *Barrington*, with No.4 boiler, on a cross-country train formed of LSWR rolling stock – possibly a Portsmouth-South Wales train between Salisbury and Westbury, c.1910.

(J.M. Bentley Collection)

TABLE 8
Pontypool Road – Shrewsbury (Bristol – Manchester express)

4119 *Wynnstay*
587 (2-4-0) to Hereford only
310 tons, 280 tons from Hereford

Distance Miles	Location	Actual mins/secs	Speed mph	Punctuality
0.0	Pontypool Road	00.00		T
6.7	Penpergwm	08.45		
9.4	Abergavenny	12.13		
13.4	Llanvihangel	20.10	26 ½	
20.9	Pontrilas	28.53		
33.4	**Hereford**	**44.25**	587 off	½ E
0.0		00.00		T
7.5	Dinmore	12.15		
12.6	Leominster	17.50		
18.9	Woofferton	24.00		
23.5	Ludlow	28.35		
28.1	Onibury	33.35		
31.1	Craven Arms	37.10		
35.6	Marsh Brook	43.12	33 minimum	
38.2	Church Stretton	47.30		
44.6	Dorrington	54.03		
51.0	**Shrewsbury**	**64.05**	sigs	1 E

3310 *Waterford*, rebuilt with a 'City' Standard No.4 boiler in 1903, at Wolverhampton alongside an Armstrong 0-4-2T, No.550, c.1905. (Bob Miller/MLS Collection)

the climbs to Onibury and to Church Stretton. The average speed from Onibury through Craven Arms to Church Stretton summit was 43.6mph and despite signal checks outside Shrewsbury station costing two minutes, the train was a minute early on arrival there.

By the end of the 1920s, the Great Western had twenty 'Kings' and forty 'Castles for their main passenger express work, with the 'Saints' and 'Stars' removing much of the work still undertaken by the double-framed 6ft 8in 4-4-0s. The final 'nail in the coffin' was the emergence of the Collett mixed

3310 *Waterford*, rebuilt with a Swindon No.4 standard boiler in November 1903, seen here on a Bristol-Paddington express, c.1904. It still retains its non-standard unique cab. (GW Trust)

3309 *Shakespeare*, with 'City' No.4 boiler, hurries through Pontrilas with a North to West express (Manchester-Shrewsbury-Bristol-Plymouth), 1910.
(J.M. Bentley Collection)

3299 *Alexander Hubbard*, after reboilering with a superheated Swindon Standard No.2 boiler in August 1911, on an up Bristol train, c.1912.
(J.M. Bentley Collection)

4104 *Cambria* (ex 3296) with a Standard No.2 boiler, heads a train of Dean four and six wheel coaches plus a horsebox on a stopping train at an unknown location, c.1913. (J.M.Bentley Collection)

4110 *Charles Mortimer* (previously 3302) now with a Swindon Standard No.2 superheated boiler runs a train of siphons with milk churns passing over water troughs on the Berks and Hants, c.1920. All 'Badmintons' by this time were equipped with super-heated No.2 boilers. (J.M. Bentley Collection/ Locomotive and General)

traffic 'Halls' in 1929. All of the large-wheeled double-framed 4-4-0s were withdrawn between 1927 and 1931, the final survivor being 4113 *Samson* which was withdrawn in May 1931 but was still intact in the scrap road of Swindon dump in October 1933.

The final allocation of the 'Badmintons' before their withdrawal was:

Tyseley (6):	4100, 4102, 4107, 4110, 4112, 4115
Bristol (6):	4103, 4105, 4106, 4108, 4109, 4117
Cardiff (2):	4104, 4116
Oxford (2):	4101, 4111
Didcot (2):	4113, 4119
Bristol SPM:	4118
Goodwick:	4114

4100 *Badminton* on a semi-fast train between Reading and London, c.1920.
(J.M. Bentley Collection)

4102 *Blenheim* (formerly 3294) at Fenny Compton on a Leamington-Banbury stopping train, 11 August 1923.
(J.M. Bentley Collection)

4106 *Grosvenor*, with No.2 boiler, superheater and topfeed with a through train from the Great Central with mixed GCR and GWR rolling stock, c.1923. (GW Trust)

4100 *Badminton*, coupled to an unidentified 'Star', ready to double-head a train to London, Wolverhampton Stafford Road, c.1925. (J.M. Bentley Collection)

4105 *Earl Cawdor,* now rebuilt with a superheated No.2 boiler, after it had its experimental S4X boiler replaced by a 'City' boiler in 1906, near Iver with a stopping train to Reading, c.1920.
(J.M. Bentley Collection/ Locomotive & General)

4105 *Earl Cawdor* at Bristol Bath Road depot with a 'Duke' behind and a 'Star' in the background, c.1925.
(GW Trust)

4111 *Marlborough* departs Paddington with a stopping train to Reading, c.1925. (GW Trust)

4111 *Marlborough* (the former 3303) fitted with superheated Standard No.2 boiler, at Reading with an Oxford – Paddington semi-fast train, c.1927. (MLS Collection)

4112 *Oxford* (ex 3304), a Tyseley engine, two years before it had its name removed, at Hatten – possibly a Birmingham-Leamington service, c.1925.
(J.M. Bentley Collection)

4109 *Monarch* (ex 3301) – a Bristol-based engine – on a stopping service which includes some Dean four-wheel coaches in its formation, c.1925.
(J.M. Bentley Collection/Real Photographs)

4109 *Monarch* pauses at Bath with a down stopping train to Bristol, 21 May 1929. *Monarch* was one of the last Badmintons to survive, being withdrawn in April 1931. (GW Trust)

4107 *Alexander Hubbard* (ex 3299), climbs Hatton bank with a Weymouth-Birmingham train, c.1925. (H.L. Salmon/J.M. Bentley Collection)

4107 *Alexander Hubbard* descends Hatton bank with a Birmingham-Leamington local service made up of Dean 4-wheeler close coupled rolling stock, c.1925. Despite this, note the locomotive is displaying the express head-lamp position.

(J.M. Bentley Collection/Real Photographs)

4106 *Grosvenor* (ex 3298) at Salisbury, having arrived on a Bristol-Portsmouth train, 17 May 1929.

(H.C. Casserley/J.M. Bentley Collection)

4119 *Wynnstay*, with superheated boiler but large copper-capped chimney, on the down Kensington-Swindon milk empties composed of GW 'siphons', c.1923. (GW Trust)

4102 *Blenheim* with an up express near Langley, c.1925. (GW Trust)

4115, unnamed, but formerly *Shrewsbury*, seen here leaving Exeter
St David's with a down express, c.1927. (GW Trust)

CHAPTER 4

THE 'ATBARAS'
DESIGN & CONSTRUCTION

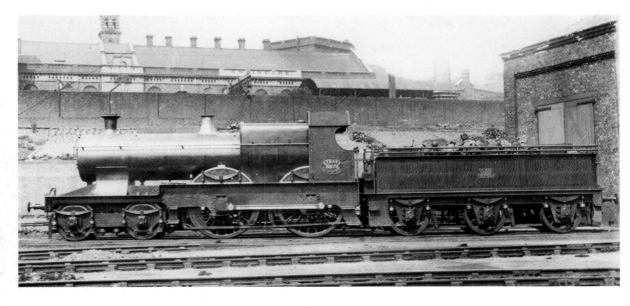

Swindon Works was building 5ft 8in 'Camels' (later referred to as 'Bulldogs') in the back half of 1899 and the start of 1900. Then from April 1900 the Works was engaged in constructing both 5ft 8in and 6ft 8in engines simultaneously. The first 6ft 8in engine appeared that month, the main difference from the 'Badmintons' being a parallel boiler with Belpaire firebox, and a straight running plate with a step behind the front bogie, removing the flowing curves of the running plate on previous designs. The cab was also wider than that on the 'Badmintons', roomy, but still giving the crew scant protection from the weather. It was the time of the Boer War and the new engines were named after personalities and locations that were in the newspaper headlines of the day (*Powerful* and *Terrible* were names of armoured cruisers involved in the conflict). Four of the express engines appeared that month and six in May before a lull when five 'Camels' were built. Then a second ten were constructed between July and September when the

production line resumed the build of 'Camels'.

The new 'Atbaras' as they became known, were named:

3373	*Atbara*
3374	*Baden Powell*
3375	*Conqueror*
3376	*Herschell*
3377	*Kitchener*
3378	*Khartoum*
3379	*Kimberley*
3380	*Ladysmith*
3381	*Maine*
3382	*Mafeking*
3383	*Kekewich*
3384	*Omdurman*
3385	*Powerful*
3386	*Pembroke*
3387	*Roberts*
3388	*Sir Redvers*
3389	*Sir Daniel*
3390	*Terrible*
3391	*Wolseley*
3392	*White*

The vital statistics of the new express engines differed little from that of the 'Badmintons', being inside

The prototype 3373 *Atbara* as built in 1900 with parallel boiler and raised Belpaire firebox, seen here at Westbourne Park depot before the building of the Old Oak Common shed in 1906.

(A.C. Gilbert/MLS Collection)

3374 *Baden Powell*, the second 'Atbara', photographed shortly after construction in 1900, and with its allocated name.3374 was the subject of several temporary renamings in the early 1900s when it was involved in a number of high profile trains, including royal and military specials.

(J.M. Bentley Collection)

cylinders 18in x 26in, slide vales with maximum travel of 4⅝in, ¾ in thick frames, 1,664.28sq ft heating surface, 180lbpsi boiler pressure, 21.28sqft grate area, with tender capacity of 3,000 gallons of water and 4 tons of coal. The axle weight over the coupled wheels was 17 tons 8 cwt and the engine weight was 51 tons 12 cwt, 84 tons 12 cwt with tender. Tractive effort at 85% was 16,010 lbs. although built with 3,000 gallon tenders, some received 3,500 or even 4,000 gallon tenders in the early years. 3385 and 3392 were equipped with Westinghouse brakes for working with rolling stock coming through from other railways. Reboilering with short and long coned boilers began in 1904 and all parallel boilers had been replaced by

1910. The coned boilers were pressed at 195lbpsi or 200lb and thus tractive effort was increased to 17,345-17,790lb. Weaknesses in the frames occurred early and as a result, strengthening measures were taken between 1905 and 1907. Early piston valves were not satisfactory and were replaced by slide valves in 1902-3.

During the popular awareness of personalities and events occurring at the time in the Boer War, the GW publicity organisation took full advantage of opportunities to promote its new engines and several of the early 'Atbaras' received temp-orary name changes in connection with high profile events – royal train journeys of the new King and Queen, and return of key military personalities. 3374 seems in

particular to have been singled out, its name being temporarily replaced by *Britannia, Kitchener, Pretoria* and *Mafeking* during the first couple of years of its life before returning permanently to *Baden Powell*. The prototype, 3373, was renamed *Maine* for a troop train special in October 1900 and *Royal Sovereign* for hauling Queen Victoria's funeral train. 3375 *Conqueror* was renamed *Edgcumbe* after only one month in service and then three years later *Colonel Edgcumbe*, using a variety of nameplate designs, and appears to have then retained that name until the end of its life. 3389 *Sir Daniel* became *Pretoria* in November 1900 after four months in service. A curious temporary renaming seems to have taken place in October 1900,

when a troop special for the 'City Imperial Volunteers' was hauled by 3392 *White*, renamed *Powerful* for the occasion. However, 3385, built only two months before 3392 was already named *Powerful*. What was the significance of this name for this train? Was it the name of the Royal Navy ship to take them to South Africa? And was 3385 not available? 3392 was the only one of this first 'lot' of 'Atbaras' to be equipped with the Westinghouse brake. Was the special made up of rolling stock with air brakes from another railway? Finally, from this group of twenty – more name changes would take place with the next 'lot' - 3376 *Herschell* lost its name at the beginning of the First World War in 1914.

A further twenty 'Atbaras' were built in 1901 and were named after countries and cities in the British Empire. They were:

3393 *Auckland*
3394 *Adelaide*
3395 *Aden*
3396 *Brisbane*
3397 *Cape Town*
3398 *Colombo*
3399 *Dunedin*
3400 *Durban*
3401 *Gibraltar*
3402 *Halifax*
3403 *Hobart*
3404 *Lyttleton*
3405 *Mauritius*
3406 *Melbourne*
3407 *Malta*
3408 *Ophir*
3409 *Quebec*
3410 *Sydney*
3411 *St Johns*
3412 *Singapore*

3374 here renamed *Britannia* prior to a royal train duty in March 1902. (J.M. Bentley Collection)

3374 *Baden-Powell* at Westbourne Park, c.1900. (GW Trust)

Another view of 3374 renamed *Britannia* for the March 1902 royal train. (J.M. Bentley Collection)

Another change of identity – 3374 here appearing as *Kitchener* at Westbourne Park, a metro 2-4-0T in the background, before hauling a special train with senior army officers involved in the Boer War, with Kitchener himself, July 1902. (J.M. Bentley Collection)

Although this 'lot' was built to the same design as the first twenty locomotives, one of them, 3405 *Mauritius*, was the subject of an experiment by Churchward in September 1902, being fitted with the first of his larger No.4 taper boilers, and thus became the prototype of the 'City' class, ten new engines of that class being built in 1903 (see Chapter 6) and a further nine of the 'Atbaras', 3400-3404 and 3406-3409 being rebuilt as 'Cities' with the Standard No.4 boiler between 1907 and 1909.

Some name changes also took place with this group of locomotives. 3394 lost its name in 1910 when a

3375 *Edgcumbe* in Works grey livery for photographic purposes – the name was later enhanced to 'Colonel Edgcumbe'. The name and numberplate are displayed together in an oval plate on the cabside as with earlier 4-4-0s. (J.M. Bentley Collection)

3375 *Edgcumbe* with an experimental type and position of nameplate above the splasher, c.1900. (J.M. Bentley Collection)

new Churchward 'Star' was named *Queen Adelaide*. 3404's name was re-spelt Lyttelton when someone presumably complained of the misspelling, although it took until 1920 for the correction to be made! And 3408 was renamed *Killarney* when it hauled the first London-Killarney Day Excursion in September 1907 and did not revert (it had been rebuilt with a 'City' boiler in May of that year). A day

3375 with its final name, *Colonel Edgcumbe*, and standard nameplate design over the splasher that was eventually adopted as the norm for GW named locomotives. (G. Tidey/Lens of Sutton/J.M. Bentley Collection)

3378 *Khartoum* with combined name and numberplate.
(G.Tidey/Lens of Sutton/J.M. Bentley Collection)

3380 *Ladysmith*, rebuilt with coned boiler at Old Oak Common shortly after its opening, c.1906.
(J.M. Bentley Collection)

A three-quarters rear view of 3381 *Maine*, giving a clear view of the then standard combined name and numberplate. (J.M. Bentley Collection)

3382 *Mafeking* before it was involved in a serious train accident at Henley-in-Arden in 1911 and was 'written off' and scrapped. (J.M. Bentley Collection)

3384 *Omdurman* with parallel boiler as built in 1900 and with 'guivered' frames c.1900. (J.M. Bentley Collection)

3384 *Omdurman*, rebuilt with a superheated Standard No.2 taper boiler, top feed and copper-cap chimney but just before the 1912 numbering, seen here at Birmingham Snow Hill, 1912. (J.M. Bentley Collection)

3385 *Powerful*, named after a battle cruiser in the Boer War fleet, with No.2 parallel boiler, and Westinghouse brake for operating with other railways' rolling stock, c.1903. (J.M. Bentley Collection/Real Photographs)

3387 *Roberts*, highly polished – 'guivered' frame, cab and tender – with No.2 parallel boiler and cast iron chimney, at Reading on an up semi-fast service, c.1901.
(J.M. Bentley Collection/Real Photographs)

3387 *Roberts*, rebuilt with a tapered No.2 boiler and copper-cap chimney, but not yet superheated or fitted with topfeed, c.1910.
(J.M. Bentley Collection/Real Photographs)

3388 *Sir Redvers* with No.2 parallel boiler as built, at Weymouth, c.1905.
(A.G. Ellis/J.M. Bentley Collection)

3390 *Terrible* – named after a British Navy Battle Cruiser – as built with parallel boiler and cast iron narrow chimney at Taunton, c.1901.
(J.M. Bentley Collection/Loco & General Photographs)

3392 *White*, the last example of the first 'lot' of twenty 'Atbaras' built in September 1900, with parallel boiler and Westinghouse brake pump, c.1905.
(J.M. Bentley Collection)

OPPOSITE PAGE:

TOP LEFT: Rear view of engine and cab of the first of the second batch of 'Atbaras', 3393 *Auckland*, c.1901.
(J.M. Bentley Collection)

TOP RIGHT: 3394 *Adelaide* as built with parallel boiler, seen here at Swindon, a Dean 4-2-2 in the background, c.1905. *Adelaide's* name was removed in 1910.
(J.M. Bentley Collection/Real Photographs)

LOWER: 3397 *Cape Town*, brand new, received at Westbourne Park, c.1901. The frame and cab of the engine has already received a 'guivering' at the hands of the cleaners.
(A.G. Ellis/J.M. Bentley Collection)

3408 *Ophir* as named when built in October 1901 and before fitting with a No.4 boiler and being renamed Killarney in 1907.
(J.M. Bentley Collection)

3410 *Sydney* rebuilt in 1910 with a superheated No.2 taper boiler (remaining as an 'Atbara') and copper-cap chimney, at Cardiff, 1912.
(J.M. Bentley Collection)

3412 *Singapore* as built with parallel boiler and narrow cast iron chimney, at Swindon, c.1901.
(J.M. Bentley Collection)

excursion sounds ambitious for the train journey to and from Fishguard and the sea crossing, and presumably one or both of the rail journeys was overnight.

At the general renumbering in 1912, the remaining 'Atbaras' were renumbered immediately after the 'Badmintons', becoming 4120-4148. 3382 *Mafeking* did not receive a new number as it was scrapped

following its damage in an accident at Henley-in-Arden in 1911 and 3400-3409 were 'Cities' by 1912 and received new numbers in the 3700 series. All the other 'Atbaras' were renumbered in sequence with just those omissions. By this time all the 'Atbaras' had been rebuilt with the No.2 Standard boiler.

By the late 1920s, Collett's 'Kings' and 'Castles' on top link main line

passenger work, and the 'Saints', 'Stars' and the new 'Halls' on other passenger and mixed traffic turns had made the 6ft 8in 4-4-0s redundant and the withdrawal and scrapping of them occurred in earnest between 1927 and 1930, with just 4132 and 4148 of the 'Atbaras' surviving into 1931, being withdrawn in April and May of that year respectively.

4120 (previously 3373) *Atbara* at Birmingham Snow Hill, 1920.
(J.M. Bentley Collection/Real Photographs)

4124 (previously 3377) *Kitchener* in the 1920s.
(J.M. Bentley Collection)

4130 (previously 3384) *Omdurman* in the 1920s. (J.M. Bentley Collection)

4138 (previously 3392) *White*, fitted with Westinghouse brake gear, c.1925. (MLS Collection)

4140 (previously 3394 *Adelaide*), after name removed in 1910 and oval combined name/numberplate replaced by the GW standard cabside numberplate, c.1920. The backing plate for the former nameplate is clearly visible. (J.M. Bentley Collection/Real Photographs)

4135 *Pretoria* (originally 3389) at Swindon, 11 September 1927. (H.C. Casserley/Author's Collection)

4141 (previously 3395) *Aden* on Swindon scrap dump, 1930.
(J.M. Bentley Collection/Real Photographs)

The last 'Atbara' survivor, 4148 (previously 3412) *Singapore* on Swindon dump in its month of withdrawal awaiting scrapping, 25 May 1931.
(J.M. Bentley Collection)

OPERATION

The 'Atbaras' in their early years took up the same type of express passenger work as their predecessors, the 'Badmintons', running from Paddington to Exeter via Bristol, London-South Wales, the North & West route between Bristol and Shrewsbury and London-Wolverhampton via Oxford and via Bicester after the cut-off opened in 1910. The 'Cities' took over the principal West of England trains from them within a year or two (see

Chapter 6) and then the 4-6-0s, the 'Stars' and 'Saints', especially from around 1912. The 'Atbaras' continued for a decade working the principal South Wales and Fishguard / Southern Ireland boat trains, having taken over from Dean '3232' class 2-4-0s.

Like the 'Badmintons', the 'Atbaras' were speedy engines and Charles Rous-Marten claimed to have timed one at 97.8mph at least two years before his recording of 100mph behind 3440. In the very first article entitled *British Locomotive Practice and Performance* written by Rous-Marten in the September 1901 edition of the *Railway Magazine* he compared maximum speeds on various railways and at that time he was particularly enthusiastic about large-wheeled singles – quoting GN Stirling singles never quite reaching 80mph, but GW broad gauge 2-2-2s timed at 81.8, Dean single 4-2-2s at 83.3, Midland Johnson singles at 84.9 – then (somewhat reluctantly) admitting an 'Atbara' 4-4-0 achieved 86mph. (He was very quiet about when and where he timed the 97.8mph.)

The first full log I have seen of an 'Atbara' in service was published in the *Railway Magazine* of September 1900, of 3374, built in April that year, on a Paddington-Birkenhead express, as far as the first stop, Leamington (via Oxford as the line via Bicester was not opened for a further ten years).

The start (into the head wind) was sluggish, but brightened up after Reading and became speedy after Oxford, when time was being

TABLE 9			
2.10pm Paddington-Birkenhead (to LeamingtonSpa), 8.8.1900			
3374 *Baden Powell*			
7 chs, 160 tons			
Driver Burnham			
(strong head/side winds throughout)			
Location	Time	Est speed	Punctuality
Paddington	00.00		T
Westbourne Park	03.18		
Southall	13.00	55	
Slough	22.20	60	
Maidenhead	28.45	60	
Reading	41.15	45*	1¼ L
Reading West Jcn	42.33		
Pangbourne	47.08	65	
Didcot East Jcn	58.25		T
Didcot North Jcn	59.15		¾ E
Oxford	69.20	68 /20*	¾ E
Wolvercote Jcn	72.35	45*	
Heyford	81.53		
Banbury	92.33		2¼ E
Fenny Compton	101.50		
Leamington (pass)	112.37	20*	4¼ E

gained. Unfortunately, the run north of Leamington was ruined by a signal check on Hatton bank, as a previous cross-country train from Bournemouth had failed ahead.

The next record I have discovered is of the outline timing of Queen Victoria's funeral train on 2 February 1902! 3373 *Atbara*, renamed *Royal Sovereign* for the occasion, departed Paddington at 1.32pm with seven royal saloons and arrived at Windsor at 2.06pm, 34 minutes for the 21 miles, which suggests that it exceeded the

3373 *Atbara*, renamed *Royal Sovereign*, prepared and ready to haul Queen Victoria's funeral train from Paddington to Windsor, February 1902.

(J.M. Bentley Collection)

3374 *Baden-Powell,* said to have been renamed *Pretoria* for a special train in connection with VIPs involved in the Boer War, but appearing to bear the name *Mafeking* (which was later applied to 3382), seen here at Plymouth, October 1900.
(J.M. Bentley Collection)

Although no exceptional high speeds were attempted, the runs in both directions were very steady with record non-stop distances involved at very remarkable economy.

The June 1902 edition of the *Railway Magazine* reported a couple of meritorious runs behind unidentified 'Atbaras'. One, hauling 170 tons, covered the Exeter-Bristol 75½ miles in 79 minutes 42 seconds (77½ minutes net) passing Whiteball summit at 52.8mph and touching 81.8 on the descent between Wellington and Norton Fitzwarren. The train stopped at Taunton, the start to stop times being 33miutes

40mph limit that Queen Victoria dictated as the uppermost speed she was prepared to tolerate on royal trains when she was alive. The funeral train was preceded by 3374 *Baden Powell* which ran light engine ahead to ensure the line was clear – it reached Windsor from Paddington in exactly 30 minutes.

Another royal train run was recorded on March 7 1902 when 3374, renamed *Britannia* for the occasion, took King Edward VII and Queen Alexandra non stop to Kingswear (228½ miles) in 262½ minutes, arriving – presumably to the embarrassment of the receiving dignitaries – some twenty minutes early at the instigation of the King who was taking a personal interest in the train's performance. Outline timings to the nearest half minute and estimated speeds are given opposite:

TABLE 10
GWR Royal Train, 7.3.1902

3374 *Britannia*
5 chs, 127/130 tons
Driver Burden

Distance	Location	Time	Ave speed (mph)	Est max speed
0.0	Paddington	00.00		
31.0	Twyford	34.00	54.8	65
36.2	Reading West Jcn	39.00	62.5	65
53.1	Didcot	56.00	59.7	55/65
77.3	Swindon	80.00	60.6	40*
106.9	Bath	110.30	58.2	70+
118.4	Pylle Hill Jcn	127.00	41.8	
137.75	Uphill Jcn	146.00	55.2	65
162.85	Taunton	171.30	59.1	60
193.6	Exeter	206.30	52.9	40/70+
213.8	Newton Abbot	234.30	43.3	
228.5	**Kingswear**	**262.30**	31.5	

Return Royal train, 10.3.1902 (same loco, load, crew)

0.0	Plymouth Millbay	00.00		
32.6	Newton Abbot	47.00	41.5	
52.8	Exeter	75.00	43.3	55/20*
83.55	Taunton	109.30	53.5	50/70+ /20*
108.65	Uphill Jcn	137.00	54.8	60
129.45	Bristol East Depot	159.30	55.5	65/30*
139.5	Bath	172.00	48.4	55/25*
169.1	Swindon	203.00	57.1	70/50
193.4	Didcot East	227.00	61.0	68
210.2	Reading West Jcn	245.30	55.5	40*
215.4	Twyford	251.00	56.8	60/68
246.4	**Paddington**	**284.00**	56.3	

42 seconds Exeter-Taunton and 43¾ minutes net Taunton-Bristol. The second run, again with the engine number unrecorded, was with the 10.35am Paddington-Falmouth. The load was 9 bogie coaches and one six-wheeler, tare weight 230 tons. The train suffered two p-way slacks before Reading which was passed in 42 minutes 37 seconds. Reading-Swindon took 42 minutes 29 seconds for the 41 miles with speed hovering between 58 and 62mph, before two p-way slacks either side of Wootton Bassett caused Bath to be passed in 117 minutes 54 seconds (113 minutes net), and Bristol Pylle Hill in 133 minutes 53 seconds. Another p-way

3387 *Roberts* heads a special troop train composed of LSWR stock to Southampton Docks, seen here passing Acton, 1902. (GW Trust)

3375 *Edgcumbe* running in after construction with a Swindon-Gloucester stopping train, at Gloucester, 1900. Shortly afterwards this engine was renamed *Colonel Edgcumbe*. (GW Trust)

3398 *Colombo* emerges from Parson's Rock Tunnel, Dawlish, on a down west of England express, c.1903.
(J.M. Bentley Collection/Loco & General Publishing Co.)

slack to 15mph at Durston meant that Taunton was passed very slowly in 180 minutes 51 seconds, then the 'Atbara' accelerated the 230 ton tare load to 40mph on the 1 in 81 with a minimum of 26.4mph at Whiteball summit. The total time to the Exeter first stop was 3 hours 38 minutes, exactly three and a half minutes net. The train was taken forward into

Devon and Cornwall by a double-headed 'Camel' and 'Duke'.

Charles Rous-Marten returned to GW performance in his articles in 1903 and published a run behind 3392 *White* on the 150 ton 2.55pm from Paddington with London well-known Driver Burden, passing Reading in 38 minutes 55 seconds at 15mph, and signal check at Moreton

Cutting but then maintaining 65-67mph on the marginally adverse grades through Shrivenham, passing Swindon in 81 minutes 46 seconds but around 78-79 minutes net. Another recorded run was with 3380 *Ladysmith* on nine coaches, 240 tons, which ran up non-stop from Exeter in 3 hours 29 minutes (107 minutes net from passing Bath) in the teeth of

3407 *Malta* leaving Dawlish with a stopping train for Newton Abbot and Kingswear, c.1905. 3407 was rebuilt with a 'City' No.4 boiler in November 1908. (GW Trust)

a side gale, with a minimum of 50mph at Whiteball, 50mph at Dauntsey and an average of 71mph from Swindon to Didcot, after which the engine was eased to avoid too early an arrival – it was three minutes early into Paddington. The driver was again a well known character, Millard. There was an interesting couple of runs in 1902 when the non-stop run to Exeter was allowed 217 minutes for the 193.6 miles, out and back with the same locomotive, 3395 *Aden*, which unusually was described by its driver as being run down, rough riding and needing overhaul. The train left London with 160 tons, three

3398 *Colombo* at an unidentified station in the west country with an express c.1903.
(J.M. Bentley Collection/Loco & General Publishing Co.)

3384 *Omdurman* leaving Manchester Exchange with a stopping train to Chester, c.1905. (GW Trust)

3403 *Hobart* pauses at Craven Arms with a Shrewsbury-Bristol express, 1904.
(MLS Collection/Bob Miller)

minutes late, and was not pressed early, barely exceeding 63mph before Reading, passed in just over 41 minutes. Then both before and after Didcot there were a series of severe signal checks causing the train to be over ten minutes late past Swindon. Rough engine or not, the delays had to be recouped and 82mph down Dauntsey bank was followed by 72 through Box Tunnel and then after Bristol the low 70s through Yatton towards Bridgwater. Then they caught another train and were brought to a dead stand before Taunton. The engine accelerated the train to 41mph through Wellington

station but fell to 29mph at the summit and twice touched 75mph on the descent to Exeter, reached five minutes late but in a net time of 203 minutes, fifteen minutes less than schedule. The return journey the next day started poorly. With a ten-coach load of 250 tons, speed fell away to 24mph on the eastbound climb to Whiteball but the driver pushed 3395 hard down the other side touching 78mph and maintaining 62mph on the levels between Taunton and Bristol, just holding the schedule to Bristol. Recovery from restrictions around Bristol and Bath was slow, but

Dauntsey was tackled with energy the nine miles from Chippenham to MP 85 taking only ten seconds over the even nine minutes, but then there was a p-way slack near Challow, signal checks after Didcot and just as speed was recovering to the upper 60s after Reading, more checks before Slough, so that arrival in London was three minutes late, the net time 214 minutes, just three minutes better than schedule.

In the summer of 1903, a number of Bristol-Paddington expresses were accelerated with non-stop trains scheduled in 125 minutes or the even two hours. Most were hauled by the

new 'City' locomotives, but one log published was of 'Atbara' 3382 *Mafeking*, which lost five minutes on a two-hour timing with a load of 175 tons, but suffered three p-way slacks and signal checks before Didcot. The high spot was a fast descent from Badminton with 75mph sustained from Hullavington to Little Somerford but the checks thereafter seemed to dishearten the driver and speed was in the low 60s through Reading to Slough until a final spurt averaging 72mph from Slough to Southall with a maximum of 75 nearly saved the day, before a final p-way slack at West London Junction. Net

3399 *Dunedin* passes Old Oak Common West with a down express for Bristol and Exeter, c.1903. (J.M. Bentley Collection/ Pouteau postcard)

'Atbara' 3400 *Durban* and a train of four clerestory coaches at an unknown location, c.1903. (J.M. Bentley Collection)

time was 118 minutes. In the down direction three runs with 'Atbaras' on heavier loads were recorded (200-230 tons) with the Bath stop reached in 116, 115 and 110 minutes net.

The *Cornish Riviera Express* was launched in 1904 and in the first week three down runs were recorded behind 'Atbara' 4-4-0s with the booked load of 6 coaches, 146 tons tare. Other motive power in that first week of the service was 102 *La France* twice and 3433 *City of Bath*. The first stop was Plymouth, 245.6

miles in 267 minutes, the 193.6 miles to passing Exeter scheduled in 197 minutes. Outline actual times are recorded opposite.

The new 'City' class locomotives were in service by this time but the 'Atbaras' were working turn and turn about with them. 3386 ran on time or ahead of schedule all the way without any exceptional effort. 3380 ran hard initially, passing Bath four minutes early having averaged 62mph start to pass with steady running in the low 70s, before easing to avoid too early an arrival. 3407 was badly checked between Slough and Reading and was six minutes late at the latter point and regained time gradually after that with a particularly fine time of thirty-one minutes for the 30.8 miles from Taunton to Exeter including the climb to Whiteball. A run in the same week in the up direction with 3386 *Pembroke* achieved the non-stop run from Plymouth in 26½ minutes,

3403 *Hobart*, before rebuilding with a 'City' boiler, with an express at an unknown location, c.1903. (J.M. Bentley Collection)

3407 *Malta*, before rebuilding with a 'City' No.4 boiler with an express at an unknown location, c.1905.
(GW Trust)

arriving 2½ minutes early with speed hovering around 70mph from Swindon to Didcot. 3407 *Malta* repeated the performance a day later.

Most of these runs were with relatively light loads, but the 10.50am Paddington was a heavier train worked by a new 4-6-0 to Bristol and a 4-4-0 on to Exeter. 3388 *Sir Redvers* had a load of 350 tons on a schedule of 85 minutes for the 75.6 miles (53.4mph). It achieved a time of one second over 82 minutes, involving 45mph up Flax Bourton bank, 72mph through Yatton, and speed in the mid 60s across the

TABLE 11
GWR Cornish Riviera Express, 1904

Load 6 chs, 146 tons tare Locomotive:		4.7.1904 3386 *Pembroke*		7.7.1904 3380 *Ladysmith*		5.7.1904 3407 *Malta*	
Distance	**Location**	**Time/Speed**		**Time/Speed**		**Time/Speed**	
0.0	Paddington	00.00		00.00		00.00	
18.5	Slough	20.00	70	20.00	70	21.00	sigs
36.0	Reading	36.00	70	37.00	65	42.00	65
53.1	Didcot	51.00	68	53.00	64	58.00	65
77.3	Swindon	75.00	65/60	76.00	67/69	82.00	65/60
106.9	Bath	104.00	70/62	102.00	75/65	109.00	72/65
118.7	Pylle Hill Jcn	118.00		117.00		123.00	
137.7	Uphill Jcn	137.00	70	134.00	75	142.00	70
162.8	Taunton	161.00	65/62	158.00	65	165.00	66
193.6	Exeter	194.00	40/70	192.00	35/65	196.00	45/75
213.7	N'ton Abbot	220.00		220.00		221.00	
245.6	**Plymouth**	**264.00**		**266.00**		**265.00**	

3412 *Singapore* passing Wormwood Scrubs with a down express just before the construction of Old Oak Common depot, c.1905. A couple of Armstrong 0-6-0 saddle tanks complete the scene. (GW Trust)

3375 *Colonel Edgcumbe* heads an express at Gloucester, c.1905. (J.M. Bentley Collection)

levels to Taunton, passed in 47 minutes 46 seconds for the 44.8 miles. A decision was taken not to seek a banker for Whiteball, so Taunton was passed at speed. This fell to 47mph by Wellington station and the final speed at the summit was 21mph – achieved without any slipping. The weather was good – a 4-4-0 with this load would not have made it in wet rail conditions. Over 70mph was reached on the descent to Exeter. On another occasion 3388 made virtually identical times with a 335 ton load. More speed recordings were made with the upper 60s across the Bridgwater levels, passing Taunton a minute quicker, but falling to 20.4mph at Whiteball summit. The 4.2 miles from Collumpton to Hele were covered at an average of

70mph and the overall time to Bristol was 82 minutes 8 seconds.

At the opposite end of the spectrum, although normally a City' turn, 3396 *Brisbane* had charge of a three-van 90 ton Ocean Mail special on 18 April 1904 and ran the 118.4 miles from Bristol Temple Meads, where crews were changed, to Paddington in 109 minutes, averaging 72½mph between Swindon and Didcot suggesting maximum speed of around 75mph, and, after a check through Reading, 67mph average on to the Paddington stop which certainly required speeds in excess of 75mph. The net time was virtually the later *Bristolian* 105 minute schedule.

In a survey carried out by A.V.Goodyear on a Summer Saturday, 2 July 1904, the following 'Badmintons' and 'Atbaras' were noted in action (shown below).

The way in which the 'Atbara' class dominated the main express trains to and from Paddington is very noteworthy. Only one 'Badminton' was seen, 3310, and that already rebuilt with a Swindon No.4 boiler, making it equal to a 'City'. It is worth remembering that by this time all the 'Badmintons' apart from 3310 and the experimental 3297 still had their original parallel boiler with Belpaire firebox. Four country based 'Atbaras' returned home the same

day, only one London based 'Atbara' and *Waterford* started from the London end and returned the same day during the observation period from 9am to 7pm. Churchward's new 4-6-0, No.98 was out and back on 2-hour Bristol expresses, 4-6-0 No.171 *Albion* appeared to be running in on a slow train from Bath and De Glehn atlantic compound 102 *La France* arrived at tea time nine minutes early with the dining car non-stop run from Plymouth. Perhaps most remarkable of all was the appearance of twenty-two (!) Dean Single 4-2-2s on Paddington departing trains – nearly all on expresses, especially to Gloucester, Worcester and Birmingham and nineteen in the up direction, of which fifteen appeared in both directions. Perhaps most remarkable of all was Dean's rebuilt 2-2-2 No.9 *Victoria*, rebuilt to the 'Queen' class in 1890 from the curious 4-2-4T of 1881 (see Chapter 1, page 8), which arrived at Paddington at 5.31pm eleven minutes late on a 7-bogie coach express from North Wales via Birmingham and was turned and returned north just an hour and a quarter later on the 6.50pm 9-bogie train to Oxford.

The 'Atbaras' performed on the boat trains to Southern Ireland working to New Milton (Neyland) until Fishguard Harbour was developed in 1907-8. A log exists of the 4.30pm Paddington-Waterford boat train, hauled to Cardiff by 'Atbara' 3410 *Sydney*. The log only commences at Bristol Stapleton Road (the recorder joined the six-coach 150 ton train at Bath) and at Cardiff

Survey of Badmintons & Atbaras at Paddington, 2.7.1904

Down direction from Paddington

Locomotive	Time	To	No. of coaches	Act dep.	Comments
3310 *Waterford*	09.00	Torquay	9 bogies	09.00½	Rebuilt as 'City'
3404 *Lyttleton*	09.50	Birmingham	11 bogies	09.51	Still Atbara class
3397 *Cape Town*	10.45	Exeter	7 bogies	10.45	1st stop Exeter
3399 *Dunedin*	11.20	South Wales	9 bogies	11.21	1st stop Newport
3392 *White*	15.03	Ilfracombe	8 bogies	15.04	1st stop Swindon
3383 *Kekewich*	15.35	South Wales	7 bogies	15.35	Express
3381 *Maine*	16.25	Irish Boat	6 bogies	16.25	3 days a week
3411 *St Johns*	16.30	Irish Boat	10 bogies	16.30	Southern Ireland
3384 *Omdurman*	18.10	South Wales	11 bogies	18.10	Express

Up Direction to Paddington

Locomotive	Time Due	From	No. of coaches	Punctuality	Comments
3383 *Kekewich*	09.55	Waterford	8 bogies +1*	15 L	Boat Train
3392 *White*	11.25	Bristol	5 bogies	7½ L	Express
3411 *St Johns*	13.00	South Wales	9 bogies	5½ L	Express
3381 *Maine*	13.10	Cork Boat	7 bogies	2 L	Stopped outside
3395 *Aden*	14.00	Bristol	7 bogies	7 L	2 hrs ex Bristol
3376 *Herschell*	15.35	Falmouth	9 bogies	T	Non-stop from Exeter
3386 *Pembroke*	16.20	South Wales	8 bogies	½ E	Express
3399 *Dunedin*	18.10	South Wales	8 bogies	20 L	Stopped outside long time
3310 *Waterford*	18.15	Ilfracombe	5 bogies +1*	5 E	Express

* 6-wheel coach

another 'Atbara', 3377 *Kitchener*, took over for the run through to New Milford Dock. The record is rare as few train timers seemed to bother to record times west of Cardiff as high speed opportunities were less. Details of speeds are scanty as the run was made in darkness and no mileposts were visible.

Fishguard Harbour was developed the following year (1907) and a Day Excursion to Killarney was run taking advantage of the new facility and night boat to Southern Ireland. The excursion train left Paddington at 8.40pm in the evening, to connect with an overnight sailing. The first run was hauled by 'Atbara' 3408 *Ophir* just rebuilt with a 'City' boiler and renamed *Killarney* for the occasion, a name it retained until its withdrawal in 1929. Then the Cunard liner *Mauretania* docked at Fishguard in 1909 and double-headed 4-4-0 specials ran the prestige boat trains to London. On the first of the specials, 3402 *Halifax*, rebuilt the previous year with a No.4 Swindon boiler, doubled-headed a 'Flower' to Cardiff. More details of the performance of the rebuilt 'Atbaras' will be given in Chapter 6.

Elsewhere the 'Atbaras' were performing sterling work, albeit out of the spotlight. One run from Chester to Pontypool Road, which had a 'County' 4-4-0 from Shrewsbury, was hauled by an 'Atbara', 3406 *Melbourne*, between Chester and Shrewsbury with a load of 242 tons. At the time (1909) 3406 had received a 'City' boiler although it was still un-superheated. It gained times on all sections, sustaining 26½mph on the four miles of 1 in 80 Gresford bank and had to run fast to maintain the 21 minute schedule for the 18 mile run from Gobowen to Shrewsbury.

A run via the opened northern route via Bicester was recorded with 3390 *Terrible* (goodness knows what the passengers who noticed made of that!), albeit with a light load of 120 tons only. The train was the 9.10am Paddington-Birkenhead, timed as far as the first stop, Leamington. It averaged 62.8mph over the adverse gradients from Denham to Beaconsfield and 75mph downhill from Princes Risborough to Ashendon Junction which suggests 80mph was exceeded. After that, it was running so early that it was eased, though not in time to avoid signal checks before Leamington station, reached in a net time of 86 minutes for the 87.3 miles.

By 1910, the GWR motive power department had 94 double-framed 6ft

TABLE 12
Waterford Boat Train, (4.30pm Paddington)-Bristol-Haverfordwest (New Milford)

3410 Sydney to Cardiff
3377 Kitchener Cardiff -New Milford
6 coaches, 150 tons

Distance Miles	Location	Time mins secs	Speed mph	Schedule
0.0	Bristol (Stapleton Rd)	00.00		T
4.3	Patchway	10.34		
7.4	Pilning	14.15		
8.9	Severn Tunnel East	16.21		
13.3	Severn Tunnel West	22.04	46mph ave.	
24.2	Newport	40.16	sigs (heavy)	
36.0	**Cardiff**	**60.03**	**3410 off**	**5 L**
0.0		00.00	**3377 on**	T L
14.0	Llanharan	19.00	colliery slack	
17.0	Pencoed	22.30		
20.8	Bridgend	26.40		¼ E
	Stormy Sdgs	-	42 estimated	
26.2	Pyle	33.48	70 estimated	
32.9	Port Talbot	40.15/41.15	sig stand	1¾ E/¾ E
38.5	Neath	52.20		2¼ L
45.0	**Landore Jcn**	**63.30**		**3½ L**
0.0		00.00	1 in 52 Cockett	1¾ L
4.8	Gowerton	13.03		5¾ L
6.9	Loughor	15.20		
10.6	Llanelly	20.00/24.05	sig stand	3¾ L/7¾ L
14.5	Pembrey	30.35		
30.3	**Carmarthen Jcn**	**50.02**		**8¾ L**
0.0		00.00		8¼ L
8.2	St Clears	12.35		
14.0	Whitland	19.10	53.5 ave	
19.4	Clynderwen	26.05	47 ave	
25.9	Clarbeston Road	33.35	52 ave /60+	
31.2	**Haverfordwest**	**39.40**		**6 L**

8in coupled 4-4-0s, 30 'County' 4-4-0s, 16 4-4-2s (including the three French compounds), 39 'Saint' 4-6-0s, 41 'Star' 4-6-0s and one pacific for its express passenger train network. After that time, they were – with the 'Badmintons' and 'Flowers' (and to a limited extent, the 5ft 8in 'Bulldogs' also) on cross-country duties, Salisbury-Cardiff, Swansea-Birmingham, Chester-Manchester and shorter distance main line semi-fast services to Weymouth, Oxford and Worcester, and Wolverhampton-Shrewsbury-Chester. They never worked west of Newton Abbot, this area being the domain of the 5ft 8in 4-4-0s before the 2-6-0s and 4-6-0s arrived on the scene. The last Wolverhampton turns to London lasted until 1923 – after that they mainly worked local services in the Leamington-Banbury-Oxford area, or semi-fast Oxford-Paddington services.

By 1905-6, some of the 'Atbaras' had been reboilered with 'City' No.4 boilers and one of the services on which they were timed was the 1.40pm Paddington non-stop to Worcester, the 120.4 miles scheduled to be run in 135 minutes (53.4mph). The train loaded a minimum of 250 tons, more in peak periods, and slipped three coaches at Kingham for the Broadway and Cheltenham branch. A regular traveller was A.V. Goodyear, who had undertaken the July Saturday survey at Paddington and O.S. Nock published three of his

3391 *Wolseley* and Dean Single 3037 *Corsair* head a southbound North & West express out of Shrewsbury past a LNWR 0-6-0ST, c.1905.
(J.M. Bentley Collection/Real Photographs)

3375 *Colonel Edgcumbe* and an Armstrong 0-6-0 double-head a stopping service, c.1903.
(J.M. Bentley Collection)

3411 *St Johns* at Worcester with an up express, c.1905.
(J.M. Bentley Collection)

runs with 'Atbaras' on this service. Two of the locomotives, 3373 *Atbara* and 3405 *Mauritius*, had been fitted with the 'City' boiler (3405 was the first to receive this boiler in 1902) but 3374 *Baden-Powell* was still fitted with the parallel boiler and Belpaire firebox as built in 1900.

3405 had a heavy load of 14 vehicles, very full, around Christmas 1906, and the effect of the strong cross-wind was equivalent to a further 80-100 tons. One further run was recorded as far as Oxford in the spring of 1914, when the 7.30pm fast to Oxford had slip portions for both Taplow and Reading. The heavy train, 340 tons gross, left Paddington and was through Southall in the

F. Moore's famous painting of No.7 *Armstrong* rebuilt with No.2 standard boiler in October 1905 and provided with a second boiler of the same type but with copper-capped chimney in 1909. Behind is 4-4-0 No.8 *Gooch*, which was not rebuilt until November 1911. The painting depicts the pair at Paddington having arrived on a double-headed train, and must represent a scene around 1910.

(F. Moore painting/postcard/M. Wrottesley Collection)

A famous colour print version of a painting copied from the photo of Dean 4-2-2 'single' 3069 *Earl of Chester* at Hayes, (see page 24). (Locomotive Publishing Company postcard Bob Miller/MLS Collection)

3304 *Oxford* on a down express at Hayes — watercolour painting by F. Moore, (see page 61).
(M. Wrottesley Collection)

3310 *Waterford*, a colour plate from the frontispiece of the February 1900 *Railway Magazine*.
(Railway Magazine/MLS Collection)

3387 *Roberts*, painted by F.Moore from a photograph, c.1910.
(M. Wrottesley Collection)

The F. Moore painting of the second *Mauretania* special waiting to draw into the Fishguard Terminus platform, with 4116 *Mignonette* ahead of 4111 *Anemone*, 30 August 1909, (see page 171).
(F. Moore/M. Wrottesley's Collection)

3440 working as a guest locomotive on the Gloucester Warwick Railway, 8 May 2005.
(MLS Collection/N.R. Knight)

A colour painting of 4107 *Cineraria* made by F. Moore, c.1908, (see page 157).
(M. Wrottesley's Collection)

A further shot of 3440 operating on the Gloucester Warwick Railway, 8 May 2005.

(MLS Collection/N.R. Knight)

3440 departs from Berwyn on the Llangollen Railway, c.2011.

(MLS Collection/Bob Miller)

TABLE 13
1.40pm Paddington-Worcester, 1905/6

Distance Miles	Location	3373 *Atbara* 250/265 tons 190t from Kingham			3374 *Baden-Powel* 298/315 tons 265t from Kingham			3405 *Mauritius* 353/380 tons 300t from Kingham		
		Time/Speed mins secs/mph			Time/Speed mins secs/mph			Time/Speed mins secs/mph		
0.0	Paddington	00.00			00.00			00.00		
5.7	Ealing	08.40			09.21			09.57		
9.1	Southall	12.10	65		12.57			13.52		
18.5	Slough	20.48	72	¼ E	21.57	65	1 L	26.21	pws	5¼ L
24.2	Maidenhead	26.17	64		27.30	63		32.41		
31.0	Twyford	32.30	66		-			39.50	57	5¾ L
36.0	Reading	37.01		2 E	39.02	60	T	44.40	63	
44.8	Goring	47.05	pws 15*		47.45	62		53.54	58	
48.5	Cholsey	50.34			51.26	65		57.55	56	
52.8	Didcot E.Jcn	54.33	60/52*	2½ E	55.30		1½ E	62.45		5¾ L
56.1	Culham	58.42			59.03	62		66.05	62	
63.4	Oxford	67.38	pws 10*	1½ E	66.25		2½ E	73.48	55	4¾ L
67.2	Yarnton	71.56			71.08			-		
76.6	Charlbury	82.00	60		81.33	58		89.27	55	
84.6	Kingham	90.30	65	3 E	89.51	pws	3¾ E	98.30		5 L
91.7	Moreton-in-M	97.31	60		98.00			106.06		
101.7	Honeybourne	108.04	62 easy		111.48	pws		115.36	66½	
106.6	Evesham	113.05		6 E	116.50		2¼ E	119.57		1 L
112.5	Pershore	119.42			124.20			125.30		
120.4	**Worcester S.H.**	**129.51**	(125 net)	**6 E**	**132.52**	(128 net)	**2¼ E**	**134.12**	(132 net)	**¾ E**

The only large-wheeled double-framed GW 4-4-0 to be completely wrecked in a train accident was 3382 *Mafeking*, which was in charge of an overnight 11pm excursion from Wolverhampton to Bristol on 25 June 1911. Because of a signalling error, the excursion was routed into the bay platform at Henley-in-Arden instead of the through road, and collided with the buffer stops at approximately 40mph, causing considerable damage and injuring eleven passengers and the train crew, though luckily there were no fatalities. The engine was deemed incapable of economic repair and was scrapped before the 1912 GW locomotive renumbering took place.

Not many logs of runs on cross-country routes of the time have been published, though I came across three timed between Cheltenham

3375 *Colonel Edgcumbe*, rebuilt with a taper No.2 standard boiler, passing Hayes, c.1910. (J.M. Bentley Collection/Pouteau postcard)

smart time of 12 minutes 28 seconds and Slough in 21 minutes 12 seconds, with speed peaking at around 66mph. Speed had dropped to 58 by Twyford, but recovered to the early 60s after Reading when the load was down to 268 tons gross. With steady running in the upper 50s from Didcot, the run to Oxford was completed in 68½ minutes. The engine was 4134 *Sir Redvers* (the former 3388 now fitted with the superheated No.2 boiler) and the driver, Peter Young. He was killed in an accident at Reading a week later when his engine, a 'County' on an up fast express, caught a glancing blow from 'Atbara' 3389 which was starting from Reading up main platform road against signals.

TABLE 14
GWR Cheltenham-Stratford-on-Avon-Birmingham Snow Hill

Distance / Location Miles		4142 *Brisbane* 110 tons Time/Speed mins secs/mph		4140 (formerly *Adelaide*) 115 tons Time/Speed mins secs/mph		4145 *Dunedin* 195 tons Time/Speed mins secs/mph		Schedule	
0.0	Cheltenham	00.00		00.00		00.00		0	
4.1	Bishop's Cleeve	05.46		05.53		-			1 in 200R
5.6	Gotherington	07.21	57	07.28	56½	-			L
9.0	Winchcombe	10.48	65	10.50		13.05	55		
11.6	Toddington	13.11		13.21		-			
16.1	Broadway	17.02	70	17.43		-	60		
18.8	Weston-sub-Edge	19.09		20.08		-			
21.1	Honeybourne East	21.00	80/60*	22.14	69/60*	24.40	70	26	1 in 150F
23.5	Long Marston	23.17	66	24.32	66	-			1 in 143/370F
26.1	Milcote	25.43	55	27.00		-	45		
29.1	**Stratford-on-Avon**	**29.15**		**30.23**		**33.55**		**30**	
0.0		00.00		00.00				0	
2.6	Wilmcote	04.31		05.07					1 in 75R
4.3	Bearley N. Jcn	06.18	65	-	65			8	
8.0	Henley-in-Arden	10.12		10.38				13	1 in 150R
12.8	Wood End Halt	16.42	42	16.12	51				1 in 150R
14.8	Earlswood Lakes	19.01		18.18					1 in 181R
17.7	Shirley	22.42		21.08				22	
20.2	Hall Green	25.19	68	23.40	64½				
21.7	Tyseley	27.22		26.05	sigs			27	
25.0	**Birmingham Snow Hill**	**32.20**		**33.58**	(31 net)			**32**	

and Birmingham Snow Hill via Stratford-on-Avon, working one of three daily services from Bristol to Birmingham via the Honeybourne route which started way back in 1908. Normally, the motive power was a 'County' 4-4-0, but three 'Atbara' runs were recorded in the *Railway Magazine* in 1926.

4142 was a real flyer with the light load averaging 75mph between Broadway and Honeybourne. Unfortunately, the timings for 4145 are very sketchy although the Winchcombe-Honeybourne time suggests 70mph was reached with the heavier load. One northbound log over the Stratford-Birmingham

3378 *Khartoum* passing Hayes with an up express, c.1910.
(J.M. Bentley Collection/Real Photographs)

3379 *Kimberley* at Parson's Tunnel, Dawlish, with a down West of England express, c.1910. (J.M. Bentley Collection)

3382 *Mafeking*, seen here shortly before its involvement in the Henley-in-Arden train crash, passing Old Oak Common on a down express, c.1910. There appears to be a locomotive trailing at the rear of the train although it is probably a chance photo of a locomotive on an adjoining line. (J.M. Bentley Collection/ Real Photographs)

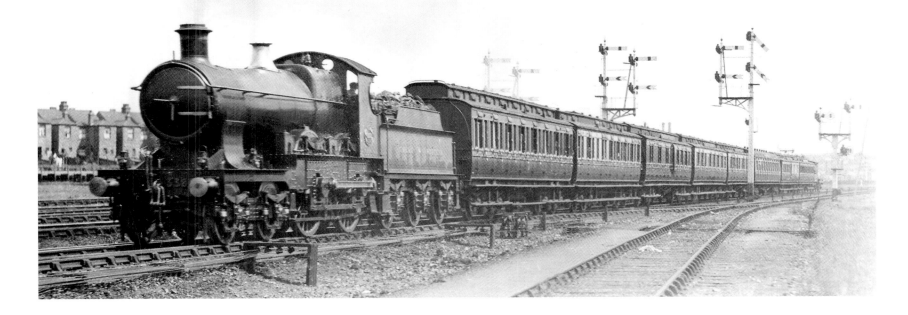

The wreck of 3382 *Mafeking* after the train crash at Henley-in-Arden, June 1911. (GW Trust)

section was recorded with 3708 *Killarney* by this date fitted with a 'City' boiler, but it had a very light load of 85 tons only. It did however sustain an average of 57mph on the long 1 in 150 gradient between Henley-in-Arden and Earlswood, to have time in hand to counter a p-way slack between Tyseley and Birmingham Snow Hill, still covering the 25 miles in the scheduled 31 minutes start to stop.

The March 1926 *Railway Magazine* published a log of one southbound run with 4147 on a heavier load, Table 15.

At the 'Big Four' amalgamation at the end of 1922, the twenty nine 'Atbaras' were distributed as follows:

Tyseley: 4120, 4126, 4132, 4140, 4142
Landore: 4121
Bristol: 4122, 4125, 4127, 4139, 4141, 4143, 4144
Cardiff: 4123, 4133, 4147
Taunton: 4124
Westbury: 4128
Old Oak Common: 4129, 4130, 4138
Goodwick: 4131
Shrewsbury: 4134
Weston-s-Mare: 4135
Wolverhampton: 4136
Swindon: 4137
Pontypool: 4145
Chester: 4146
Worcester: 4148

It is surprising that so many sheds just had one example, but one must remember that by 1922 the 'Badmintons', 'Atbaras', 'Flowers', and 'rebuilt Armstrongs', all numbered in the 41XX series, were treated as identical locomotives for operating purposes, so most of these

TABLE 15
Birmingham Snow Hill-Cheltenham Malvern Road

4147 St Johns
171/180 tons

Mileage	Location	Time	Speed	Schedule	
0.0	Birmingham S.H	00.00		0	
3.3	Tyseley	05.56	30*	5	
4.8	Hall Green	08.35			
7.3	Shirley	11.50	51		1 in 183R
10.2	Earlswood Lakes	15.16			1 in 181F
14.0	Danzey	19.03	68		1 in 150F
17.0	Henley-in-Arden	21.48	70*	20	1 in 150F
20.7	Bearley N Jcn	25.14		24	
22.4	Wilmcote	27.00			1 in 180R/ 1 in 75F
25.0	**Stratford-on-Avon**	**30.30**		**31**	
0.0		00.00		0	
3.0	Milcote	04.44			
5.6	Long Marston	07.32			
8.0	Honeybourne E Jcn	10.07	50*	10	1 in 143R
10.3	Weston-sub-Edge	12.31	54		
13.0	Broadway	15.19	63		1 in 200R
17.5	Toddington	19.52			L/1 in 150R
20.1	Winchcombe	22.26	57½		
23.5	Gotherington	25.51			L/1 in 150F
25.0	Bishop's Cleeve	27.30			
29.1	**Cheltenham Malv. Rd**	**32.21**		**33**	

A rare photograph of an 'Atbara', 3384 *Omdurman*, at Victoria station in London, having worked an excursion train from Birmingham and Wolverhampton, c.1910.
(J.M. Bentley Collection)

3393 *Auckland* leaving Paddington with a down express, c.1910. 3393 has just been equipped with a superheated No.2 standard boiler and copper-capped chimney.
(GW Trust)

3408 *Ophir* fitted with a Swindon No.4 boiler, at Kingswear, c.1907.
(MLS Collection)

sheds had other engines of those classes also.

Towards the end of the 1920s as their use was rendered redundant by the cascade of 'Saints', 'Stars' and moguls and the new 'Halls' (from 1929), they graduated to freight work, especially around Banbury –

4138 *White* of Old Oak Common was used exclusively on freight from 1927 until its demise in November 1929. On the whole, however, they finished their days on stopping passenger services or light semi-fast trains, and few if any logs are available of runs behind 'Atbaras' in

the 1920s as they worked few trains demanding significant effort or speed. At the end they were still widely distributed around the system, their final allocations being:

Tyseley: 4126, 4127, 4132, 4143, 4147
Chester: 4139
Leamington: 4120

3397 *Cape Town*, equipped with a Swindon No.4 boiler, at Bristol Temple Meads, c.1909. (J.M. Bentley Collection/Loco & General Publishing Co.)

4130 *Omdurman*, shortly after renumbering, rebuilt with standard No.2 superheated boiler, topfeed and copper-capped chimney, leaving Paddington on a down express, c.1912. (GW Trust)

4123 *Herschell*, equipped with superheated No.2 boiler on an up express leaving Sonning Cutting, c.1912. (GW Trust)

4120 *Atbara* (formerly 3373), on a local train of Dean 4-wheel coaches in the south Birmingham suburbs, c.1920. (J.M. Bentley Collection)

Shrewsbury: 4129
Banbury: 4136
Bristol: 4121, 4125, 4135 (SPM)
Westbury: 4137, 4145
Salisbury: 4140, 4141, 4146
Didcot: 4124, 4130, 4131
Swindon: 4128
Old Oak Common: 4138
Cardiff: 4123, 4133, 4134
Landore: 4122, 4142
Goodwick: 4144
Severn Tunnel Jcn: 4148

Apart from 3382 withdrawn before renumbering after accident damage in 1911, and the ten 'Atbaras' rebuilt as 'Cities', the rest of the class lasted until 1927, ten being withdrawn that year, seven the following year, six in 1929, four in 1930, leaving the last two, 4132 of Tyseley and 4148 of Severn Tunnel as the final survivors, both withdrawn in the spring of 1931.

The Westinghouse-fitted 'Atbara' 4138 *White* on an up express at Reading, c.1920. (J.M. Bentley Collection/M.W. Earley)

4142 *Brisbane* at Birmingham Snow Hill, c.1920. (J.M. Bentley Collection/W.L. Good)

4128 *Maine* heads a Birmingham-Paddington express past Bentley Heath, c.1923. (GW Trust)

4148 *Singapore* at Worcester, c.1925.
(J.M. Bentley Collection)

4136 *Terrible* heads a freight towards Hinksey Yard, Oxford, near Appleford, c.1920.
(GW Trust)

CHAPTER 5

THE 'CITIES'

DESIGN & CONSTRUCTION

'Atbara' 3405 *Mauritius* after rebuilding with No.4 tapered boiler in September 1902. (J.M. Bentley Collection/Real Photographs)

Another view of 3405 *Mauritius* after rebuilding with Churchward's first No.4 standard boiler seen here is the GW standard 3,000 gll tender, c.1905. (J.M. Bentley Collection)

The first 'City' was an 'Atbara' – Churchward rebuilt 3405 *Mauritius* as early as September 1902 with a larger Standard No.4 boiler, pressed at 200lbpsi and a total heating surface of 1,818.12sqft. 3405 had been one of the 'Atbaras' built in 1901 with a parallel boiler and Belpaire firebox. Churchward gave a paper to the Institution of Mechanical Engineers in February 1906 which included his reasons for the development of the tapered boiler, building heavily on his experience of American locomotive practice. He had been particularly impressed with larger boilers' ability to improve water circulation, especially at the rear near the back tube-plate. Churchward continued to develop his own version, retaining the Belpaire firebox and having the coning of the boiler, unlike American practice, at the rear. The flat top of the firebox also increased the water space available on the hottest part of the boiler. Having earlier experimented with new type boilers incorporating his ideas on 5ft 8in 3312 *Bulldog* and 6ft 8in 3310 *Waterford*, he was ready to introduce the fully developed boiler on 3405.

3440 *City of Truro* as built in Works Grey, with 3,000 gallon tender and coal fender, 1903.
(GW Trust)

The rebuilt engine had an increased tractive effort of 17,790lb and was evidently successful enough for Churchward to get the GW Board to authorise the construction of ten similar new engines, which were almost identical – a slightly reshaped Belpaire firebox being the main visual difference. This boiler was developed at the same time as the Swindon Standard No.1 boiler, being fitted on Churchward's contemporary 4-6-0s. Initially, their tenders had coal rails but most later had 3,500 gallon tenders with fenders. The 'Cities' were built with narrow cast-iron chimneys but these were replaced with larger diameter copper-cap chimneys between 1907 and 1909. These new 4-4-0s were delivered from Swindon Works in 1903, numbered 3433-3442 and were named after cities on the GWR system as follows:

3433 *City of Bath*
3434 *City of Birmingham*
3435 *City of Bristol*
3436 *City of Chester*
3437 *City of Gloucester*
3438 *City of Hereford*
3439 *City of London*
3440 *City of Truro*
3441 *City of Winchester*
3442 *City of Exeter*

3434 *City of Birmingham* running in after construction with a Gloucester-Swindon stopping train at Gloucester, 1903.
(J.M. Bentley Collection/Loco & General Photographs)

The first 'City' 3433 *City of Bath*, shortly after construction, with the 3,000 gallon tender fitted with coal rails, 1903.
(J.M. Bentley Collection)

3436 *City of Chester* at Swindon loco depot shortly after construction, 1903.
(J.M. Bentley Collection)

3437 *City of Gloucester* at Westbourne Park, c.1903. (J.M. Bentley Collection/Real Photographs)

The last locomotive, *City of Exeter*, is out of line in that the GW tended to stick to alphabetical order in its locomotive naming policy. One might have therefore expected 3442 to be *City of Worcester* (although a Dean 'Single' was named *Worcester*) – there is therefore a suspicion that a faux-pas had been made and Exeter omitted in error – and hastily corrected at Worcester's expense!

With the success of 3405 in 1902 and the spectacular introduction of the newly built 'City' class (see the 'Operations' section of this chapter, page 139) it was decided to authorise the equipping of further 6ft 8in 4-4-0s with the No.4 boiler, in effect increasing the class of 'Cities'. All the 'Badmintons' bar three (3301, 3302 and 3304) were thus equipped between 1904 and 1906, until it was found that the large boiler was too heavy for their frames and they had reverted to the lighter Standard No. 2 boiler by 1911. However, another nine 'Atbaras' of the same series as *Mauritius* received the No.4 boiler between 1907 and 1909 and became

3433 *City of Bath* at Old Oak Common, by then fitted with copper-cap chimney instead of the narrow cast-iron model, c.1908. (GW Trust)

3435 *City of Bristol*, 12 July 1905. (GW Trust)

officially classified as 'Cities' rather than rebuilt 'Atbaras'. These rebuilds retained their original numbers until the 1912 general renumbering and were the following:

3400	*Durban* rebuilt	4/07
3401	*Gibraltar*	2/07
3402	*Halifax*	12/08
3403	*Hobart*	2/09
3404	*Lyttleton**	10/07
3406	*Melbourne*	1/08
3407	*Malta*	11/08
3408	*Killarney*	5/07
3409	*Quebec*	11/07

* (re-spelt *Lyttelton* later)

The frames of the ten locomotives built in 1903 as 'Cities' were strengthened between 1904-6 to

'Atbara' 3401 *Gibraltar* at Swindon Works under conversion to 'City' class by equipping with a No.4 standard boiler, February 1907.
(J.M. Bentley Collection)

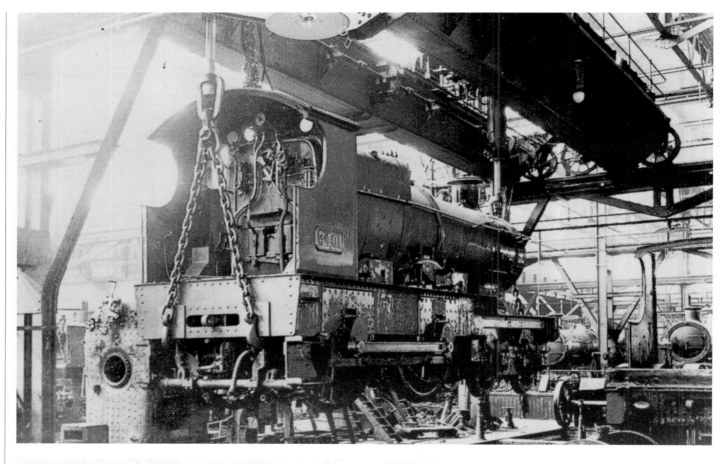

Rebuilt 'Atbara' 3401 *Gibraltar* on a depot in the Wolverhampton Division with a 36XX 2-4-2T and a Armstrong 0-6-0, c.1910.
(GW Trust)

obviate the frame problems experienced by the Badmintons. Most had steam reversing gear, though a few later had screw reverse.

The 'City' boilers were superheated between 1910 and 1912, the first so equipped being 3402. Top feed was developed and implemented also from 1911. Under the general renumbering in 1912, the 4-4-0s with No.4 boilers were all renumbered in the 37XX series while all the double-framed 4-4-0s with the Standard No.2 or 3 boiler were put together in the 41XX series of

Rebuilt 'Atbara' 3408 *Ophir* before renaming, 1907. (J.M. Bentley Collection)

Rebuilt 'Atbara' 3408 after renaming *Killarney* to mark the running of GW's first day excursion to Southern Ireland on the Autumn of 1907. 3408 retained this intended temporary name for the rest of its life. (J.M. Bentley Collection)

Rebuilt 'Atbara' 3402 *Halifax* at Reading, with top feed, c.1911.
(J.M. Bentley Collection)

Side view of rebuilt 'Atbara' 3407 *Malta* at Reading station, c.1910.
(J.M. Bentley Collection/Loco & General Photographs)

numbers. Thus, 3400 -3409 became 3700-3709, with 3433-3442 becoming 3710-3719.

By the end of the First World War the 'Cities' had been superseded on the main line top link work by the now numerous 4-6-0s and were retained without significant change through the 1920s before their early retirement in the late 1920s along with all the other express double-framed 4-4-0s. Although more powerful than the 'Badmintons', 'Atbaras' or 'Flowers', they were redundant and were all withdrawn between 1927 and 1931, apart from 3717 *City of Truro*, which, because of its claim to fame as Britain's first 100mph locomotive, found a place in the old York Railway Museum.

3437 *City of Gloucester* at Gloucester station running in after construction, 1903. (J.M. Bentley Collection/Loco & General Photographs)

The first 'Atbara' 1902 rebuild, 3705 (ex 3405) *Mauritius*, shortly after renumbering, on shed, c.1912. (GW Trust)

Rebuilt 'Atbara' 3700 *Durban*, formerly 3400, shortly after the 1912 renumbering, at Bristol Temple Meads, c.1913. (J.M. Bentley Collection/Loco & General Photographs)

Close-up side view of rebuilt 'Atbara' 3704 (ex 3404) *Lyttelton*, with 'Aberdare' type chimney, c.1913. (J.M. Bentley Collection/Real Photographs)

Rebuilt 'Atbara' 3705 *Mauritius* (ex 3405), c.1923. (J.M. Bentley Collection/Real Photographs)

3719 *City of Exeter*, c.1925. (J.M. Bentley Collection/Real Photographs)

Rebuilt 'Atbara' 3709 (ex 3409) *Quebec*, c.1925. (J.M. Bentley Collection/Moore's Postcard)

Rebuilt 'Atbara' 3702 (ex 3402) *Halifax* at Reading depot, c.1925. (J.M. Bentley Collection)

3714 *City of Gloucester* at Oxford, c.1925. (MLS Collection/A.G. Ellis)

3712 *City of Bristol*, c.1925. (J.M. Bentley Collection)

Rebuilt 'Atbara' 3706
Melbourne, c.1925.
(J.M. Bentley Collection/Real
Photographs)

3716 *City of London* at
Old Oak Common,
c.1925. (J.M. Bentley
Collection/Real Photographs)

Rebuilt 'Atbara' 3701 *Gibraltar*, shortly before withdrawal, c.1927. (J.M. Bentley Collection)

Rebuilt 'Atbara' 3702 (ex 3402) *Halifax* at Swindon shortly before withdrawal, c.1927. (J.M. Bentley Collection/Real Photographs)

3712 *City of Bristol*, at Reading shed, 23 August 1930. (J.M. Bentley Collection)

3712 *City of Bristol* being broken up at Swindon Dump, 14 June 1931. The last 'Atbara' 4148 Singapore awaits the same fate. (GW Trust)

OPERATION

The new 'Cities' rapidly took over the prestige West of England expresses from the 'Badmintons' and 'Atbaras' and enjoyed spectacular success between their introduction in 1903 and the end of the decade, by which time they in turn were being displaced by Churchward's 'Saints' and 'Stars'. The first ten newly built 'Cities' were all allocated immediately to the Paddington-West of England services, six at Westbourne Park (Paddington), three at Exeter and one at Bristol Bath Road. The rebuilt 'Atbara', 3405, was based at Cardiff.

Their days of glory included royal train duties arousing the interest of King Edward VII, and, as is well-known, the Plymouth-London Ocean Mail specials that developed into a competition with the LSWR in 1904, culminating in 3440 *City of Truro's* claimed 102mph down Wellington Bank. That exploit and Rous-Marten's timings have been pored over so many times inconclusively, that it seems that we shall never know for certain whether the magic 100mph was reached – it seems to depend on the investigator's natural bias with O.S. Nock supporting the achievement and Cecil J. Allen sceptical, leaving *Flying Scotsman* to claim the first authenticated 100mph by a steam locomotive in Great Britain. A postal worker in the Mail train also timed the train with a stop watch claiming a 100mph speed over two successive readings and a later Rous-Marten timed run with another 'City'

recorded 95½mph with identical times from Whiteball to Taunton but without the emergency slowing to 80mph after Wellington that Rous-Marten reported, so 100mph does look likely, even if the claimed 102.3 is on the high side. Whatever the actual figure, it certainly exceeded any other European locomotive of the first decade of the twentieth century, the nearest being the Bavarian Railway's unique 4-4-4 No.3201 which reached 94½mph and was Germany's fastest until the 1930s. There are rumours – started by senior engineers at Swindon – of a spectacular, nay, foolhardy, light engine run by a Churchward 'Saint' on test, 2903, down through Hullavington, when 120mph was reported, but there are no records to test this claim.

'Atbara' 3374 had performed a highly publicised triumph for the new King's benefit in 1902 and in July 1903 an even more spectacular royal run was made with the new 3433 for the Prince and Princess of Wales' tour of South Devon. The royal saloons were attached to the regular *Cornishman* express and the train ran very early, rumoured to the extreme embarrassment of the VIP reception party who were not ready for the arrival. Unlike some high speed races to Scotland by competing East and West Coast expresses in the 1890s, no risks were taken and the run was very smooth with much of the journey on the level run very steadily in the mid-seventies.

The 'Cities' made their reputation with their highly publicised performances on the Ocean Mails

TABLE 16
Paddington-Plymouth with Royal Saloons for the Prince of Wales

10.40am Paddington-Plymouth *Cornishman*
3433 *City of Bath*
130 tons

Distance	Location	Time	Ave. Speed	Estimated Max/Min
0.0	Paddington	00.00		
1.3	Westbourne Park	02.47		
5.7	Ealing Broadway	07.32	53.7	
9.1	Southall	10.35	66.9	
13.2	West Drayton	14.13	67.7	
16.2	Langley	16.42	72.4	
18.5	Slough	18.35	73.3	75
24.2	Maidenhead	23.26	70.5	
31.0	Twyford	29.14	70.3	
36.0	Reading	33.26	71.5	
38.7	Tilehurst	35.43	70.9	
41.5	Pangbourne	38.07	72.4	
44.8	Goring	40.47	71.9	
48.5	Cholsey	43.50	72.8	
53.1	Didcot	47.33	74.4	
60.4	Wantage Road	53.40	71.6	
66.5	Uffington	58.56	69.5	
71.6	Shrivenham	63.12	71.8	
77.3	Swindon	68.01	71.1	
82.9	Wootton Bassett	72.44	71.3	
87.7	Dauntsey	76.31	76.0	87½
94.0	Chippenham	81.10	81.3	
98.3	Corsham	84.54	68.8	
101.9	Box	87.41	77.4	
104.6	Bathampton	89.55	72.4	
106.9	Bath	92.02	62.8	
111.4	Saltford	96.41	57.4	
113.8	Keynsham	98.44	70.6	
117.0	Bristol East Depot	101.52	61.2	
118.7	Pylle Hill Jcn	104.42	27.6	
124.0	Flax Bourton	110.46	52.6	
130.0	Yatton	115.45	72.2	
142.2	Brent Knoll	125.24	76.0	83½
145.0	Highbridge	127.36	76.4	
151.3	Bridgwater	132.45	73.4	
162.8	Taunton	142.39	69.7	
164.8	Norton Fitzwarren	144.58	52.0	
169.9	Wellington	150.03	60.2	
173.7	Whiteball Box	154.27	51.8	50
178.7	Tiverton Jcn	158.58	66.5	
181.0	Collumpton	160.57	69.6	
190.2	Stoke Canon	169.12	66.9	
193.6	Exeter	172.34	60.8	
198.3	Exminster	178.32	47.2	
202.1	Starcross	181.54	67.6	
205.8	Dawlish	185.32	60.9	
208.6	Teignmouth	190.15	35.4	
213.8	Newton Abbot	195.51	55.7	
217.7	Dainton Box	201.28	40.6	32
222.5	Totnes	206.46	54.4	
227.0	Rattery Box	213.24	40.7	36
229.3	Brent	216.12	49.3	
231.5	Wrangaton	218.45	51.7	
238.9	Hemerdon Box	226.24	58.0	
241.6	Plympton	228.54	64.8	
245.6	**Plymouth North Rd**	**233.35**		

3435 *City of Bristol* with a Bristol-London express passing Twerton station, near Bath, c.1905.
(MLS Collection)

TABLE 17
Exeter-Bristol, Ocean Mails 1904

Distance	Location	3442 City of Exeter 5 vans, 150 tons 9.4.1904			3440 City of Truro 5 vans 148 tons 9.5.04		
		Time/Ave speed	Max/min		Time/Ave speed	Max/min	
0.0	Exeter	00.00			00.00	30* pass	
1.3	Cowley Bridge Jcn	02.40			-		
3.5	Stoke Canon	-			03.52	54.4	
7.2	Silverton	-			07.24	62.9	
8.4	Hele	-			08.31	64.5	
12.6	Collumpton	-		72	12.11	68.8	70
14.9	Tiverton Jcn	15.02	66.0	62	14.30	59.8	58
19.2	Burlescombe	-		72	18.41	61.6	64
19.9	Whiteball Box	19.30	67.1	60	19.29	53.5	50
	MP 173	-			20.24	65.7	77
	MP 172	-			21.06	85.7	94
	MP 171	-			20.43	96.0	100-102 est
23.7	Wellington	23.02	64.7	75/87	21.16	89.2	85*
28.8	Norton Fitzwarren	-		92	25.17	76.5	80
30.8	Taunton	27.55	87.1	75	26.49	78.2	65*/70
36.6	Durston	-			31.40	71.6	75
42.3	Bridgwater	36.42	78.5	80	36.08	76.5	78
48.6	Highbridge	-			41.07	57.7	
55.9	Uphill Jcn	47.24	76.3		-		
63.6	Yatton	53.35	74.7		52.59	75.9	76
69.6	Flax Bourton	-		70/77	58.09	69.7	65/75
74.5	Bedminster	62.30	73.4		62.17	70.9	
75.6	**Bristol Temple Meads**	**65.24**			**63.17**	**74.9**	**Pylle Hill Jcn**

although the most spectacular element – the 100mph claim – was suppressed for a number of years. Initially the 'Cities' powered the specials from Plymouth to Bristol with Dean 'Singles' covering the Bristol-London leg. However, the GW authorities soon gained sufficient confidence in the new engines to roster them right through to London without engine change. In the table below are two of the most well-known runs when the engine change at Bristol still took place.

I have estimated the maximum and minimum speeds in the table above using the figures quoted by Rous-Marten as guidelines together with the average speeds and gradient profiles.

The 'Cities' were not just masters of the easier gradients east of Exeter. *City of Truro* on its record journey had run from Plymouth Millbay to passing Newton Abbot, 32.7 miles in 36 minute 42 seconds. This involved 70mph through Plympton falling to 27mph at the summit of Hemerdon Bank's 1 in 42, a lively 65mph at Wrangaton and an even livelier 77mph down Rattery Bank gaining impetus for the climb to Dainton, averaging 57.5mph from Totnes to Dainton summit cleared at well over 30mph. 3442 *City of Exeter,* one of the favourites for the Ocean Mails, cleared the Plymouth-Newton Abbot section in roughly the same time on 30 April, 3437 *City of Gloucester* the same again on 2 May. 3437 worked right through to Paddington on that occasion and 3442 did also on 7 May, the two engines covering the 118.7 miles from Pylle Hill Junction in 106

3433 *City of Bath* at Plymouth after arrival on its spectacularly early arrival of the royal train carrying the Prince of Wales, 1903.
(J.M. Bentley Collection)

and 110½ minutes respectively, with sustained speeds in the mid-70s east of Swindon. On another undated run, timed by Rous-Marten with an unidentified 'City', he claimed 25½mph minimum at Hemerdon, 37½ at Dainton, 56 at Whiteball and a full 95½mph on the unchecked descent of Wellinton Bank, matching 3440's 100mph time from Whiteball to Taunton.

The 'Cities' held sway on the fastest GW expresses in the first decade of the twentieth century until displaced by the 4-6-0s which matched their times with heavier

3433 *City of Bath* on an express at an unknown location, c.1905. (GW Trust)

3442 *City of Exeter* departing Teignmouth with a Plymouth-Paddington express, c.1906. (MLS Collection)

loads. 3433 *City of Bath* gained seven minutes on the 112 minute schedule to passing Bath (106.9 miles) on the 230 ton 10.45 Paddington-Bristol (Bath was passed at slow speed where a slip coach was detached) with sustained running in the mid-upper 60s from Slough to Swindon. One fast train regularly hauled by a 'City' was the 12 noon Bristol-Paddington non-stop. A couple of clergymen, Rev W.J. Scott and Rev W.A. Dunn, logged this train with

three 'Cities' and 3382, an 'Atbara' that did not survive the 1911 Henley-in-Arden train crash. With loads varying from 150-165 tons, the three 'Cities', 3435 *City of Bristol* (twice) and 3437 *City of Gloucester* made net times of 109½, 110 and 115 minutes against the schedule of two hours. All three runs were heavily delayed by p-way slacks and, in a couple of cases, by signal checks, one run early, one run nearly on time and the fast net time recording an actual

arrival nine minutes late. This run, between the checks, sustained 69-73mph between Didcot and Reading and 75mph from Maidenhead until after Slough. All three runs had sustained running in the low 70s on the level.

A run with 3437 on the 3pm Paddington non-stop to Exeter, schedule 210 minutes for the 193.6 miles via Bristol, reached Exeter on time, but with a net time of only 188 minutes, load 150 tons. 78mph was reached down Dauntsey bank and speed was in the upper 60s between Bristol and Taunton, but a bad check to 20mph at Wellington was followed by 31mph on the steepest part of the bank with a recovery to 35mph at Whiteball summit, and a high speed of 83mph before Exeter. The following day, 27 April 1904, just a fortnight before its historic run, 3440 was timed on the 12.07pm up Torquay express, non-stop from Exeter in the same three and a half hour schedule. The load was much heavier, ten coaches for 260 tons, with Whiteball topped at 33mph, 77mph on the descent, but nothing over 70mph on to London. 3442 *City of Exeter* with 230 tons did the run in 200 minutes net with similar speeds either side of Whiteball but much faster running – at sustained 75mph – east of Swindon.

After the spectacular running on the West of England trains for the first two or three years of their existence, they were gradually replaced by the 4-6-0s and were found on the Fishguard/Irish boat trains and, after 1910, on the accelerated two-hour lightweight London-Birmingham expresses. Rous-Marten timed the first overnight 'day' excursion to Killarney in 1907, hauled throughout to Fishguard by rebuilt 'Atbara' 3408, renamed *Killarney* for the occasion. With a load of 180 tons, 3408 passed Reading in 36¼ minutes in the low 70s, was just inside even time at Swindon with speed up the Vale of the White Horse hovering around the 64-65 mark, but thereafter timing was sketchy in the

An unidentified 'City' on a Newbury race special near Acton – the South Harrow District Line and signalbox is seen in the background, c.1908. (J.M. Bentley Collection)

3434 *City of Birmingham* enters Paddington station with an express, c.1908. (GW Trust)

3434 *City of Birmingham* awaits departure from Paddington with a down express, c.1910.
(J.M. Bentley Collection)

3441 *City of Winchester* passing Acton on an up express, c.1910.
(MLS Collection/Pouteau postcard)

darkness, though an average of 56.5mph was made from Wootton Bassett to Badminton. Cardiff was passed in 153 minutes from London and Fishguard was eventually reached in just under the five hours, five minutes early. Another 'Atbara/City' rebuild, 3402 *Halifax*, piloting a 'Flower', 4108 *Gardenia*, hauled the inaugural ten-coach Fishguard *Mauretania* special in 1909, the pair reaching Cardiff eleven minutes before schedule (131 minutes for the 116 miles scheduled in 142 minutes). Despite the undulating nature of the railway, the pair timed the train at 82mph east of Clarbeston Road, but fell to

19½mph on the 1 in 50 two mile climb to Cockett.

At this time several of the 'Badmintons' had received No.4 standard boilers, and were in effect 'Cities' and were timed on the North & West route, albeit with relatively light loads. 3311 *Wynnstay* with just 100 tons took 61 minutes for the 51 miles and 3300 *Hotspur* with 175 tons took 63 minutes for the northbound Hereford-Shrewsbury section, arriving five minutes early. The 'Badminton / City' conversion was short-lived, however, with their replacement of Standard No.2 boilers

The first 1902 'Atbara' rebuild, 3405 *Mauritius*, passing Slough with a Bristol-Paddington express, c.1910. (GW Trust)

3441 *City of Winchester* passing Southall with a Paddington-Oxford express, c.1910. (GW Trust)

Rebuilt 'Atbara' 3403 *Hobart* passing Old Oak Common West with a down express, c.1910. (GW Trust)

Rebuilt 'Atbara' 3406 *Melbourne* at speed with an express at an unidentified location, c.1910. (J.M. Bentley Collection)

Rebuilt 'Atbara' 3409 *Quebec* passing Slough on a down express, c.1908. (GW Trust)

Rebuilt 'Atbara' 3701 (ex 3401) *Gibraltar* at Shrewsbury with a local Wolverhampton-Chester train, c.1912. (GW Trust)

to save stress on the frames. Another 'temporary City', 3298 *Grosvenor*, ran a Leamington-Paddington express in 92 minutes as recorded in the chapter on 'Badmintons' (page 67) and 3406 Melbourne, an 'Atbara' that retained its No.4 boiler and was reclassified as a 'City' achieved a time of 88 minutes for the 87.3 miles from Leamington to Paddington with a load of 180 tons. The best bit of the run was the ascent of Saunderton bank, averaging 58.8mph over seven adversely graded miles, the minimum at the summit being 55mph. The run was completed three minutes before time.

Rebuilt 'Atbara' 3704 *Lyttelton* (ex 3404) with 'Aberdare' style chimney, with a cross-country train composed of LSWR rolling stock, c.1920. (GW Trust)

Rebuilt 'Atbara' 3704 *Lyttelton* at Slough, with orthodox chimney restored, c.1923. (GW Trust)

After the First World War, the allocation of the twenty 'Cities' had changed completely. Only one was in the West of England – a solitary example at Taunton, that was used on stopping services to Westbury or Exeter or on the Barnstaple branch. Two more were at Westbury, working to Bristol, Taunton or Salisbury. The majority, nine, had graduated to the Wolverhampton motive power division, with four at Stafford Road, three at Chester, and one each at Shrewsbury and Banbury. Some were working the lightweight Birmingham-Paddington services via both Bicester and Oxford, but the majority

Rebuilt 'Atbara' 3708 *Killarney* at speed with an express at an unidentified location, c.1923. (GW Trust)

3711 *City of Birmingham* on an up Birmingham-London express near Bentley Heath, c.1920. (GW Trust)

Rebuilt 'Atbara' 3706 *Melbourne* at Appleford with a mixed passenger/parcels train for Paddington, c.1923. (GW Trust)

3713 *City of Chester* with a Paddington-Birmingham express on Lapworth troughs, c.1923. (GW Trust)

of their work was on semi-fast or stopping passenger work in the Leamington-Birmingham-Shrewsbury-Chester area. The next largest contingent was in the London division, with four at Oxford and two at Reading performing semi-fast and stopping services between Oxford, Reading and Paddington, or Oxford-Banbury and Leamington. This general distribution changed little throughout the 1920s, although individual engines changed sheds.

Most 'City' recorded logs are of their earlier 'glory' days when they were involved on spectacular runs on royal trains and Ocean Mail specials. At the end of the 1920s, as the end of their lives approached, little had changed from the situation a decade

3713 *City of Chester* leaving Paddington with
a Birmingham express, c.1923. (GW Trust)

3719 *City of Exeter* with an express at an unidentified location, c.1923. (GW Trust)

3718 *City of Winchester* on an up express on the Relief line passing Twyford, c.1923. (GW Trust)

earlier in either allocation or work. They had by then all left the West of England and the majority – twelve – were based in the Wolverhampton motive power division – three at Stafford Road, three at Chester, two at Shrewsbury, two at Leamington and two at Banbury. Bristol had just two, the rest being used on outer London services, based at Oxford (four), Reading (one) and Old Oak Common (one).

However, one run of a Wolverhampton division engine on a humdrum duty typical of their activity in the last few months before withdrawal was recorded by G.J. Aston and is held in the archives of the Railway Performance Society. It just covers a snippet from Oxford to

3711 *City of Birmingham* at Hatton with an express for Paddington, c.1923. (J.M. Bentley Collection/W.L. Good)

3711 *City of Birmingham* near Knowle with a London-Birmingham train, September, 1929.
(J.M. Bentley Collection/ W.L. Good)

Rebuilt 'Atbara' 3708 *Killarney* leaves Shrewsbury with a stopping train for Hereford, c.1925.
(GW Trust)

Banbury (timed to the nearest five seconds) and is included here to give a flavour of the everyday working in their latter years.

TABLE 18			
Oxford-Banbury, 28 February 1929			

3713 *City of Chester*
8 coaches & 3 vans, 245 tons tare

Mileage	Location	Time	Speed
0.0	Oxford	00.00	
2.9	Wolvercote Jcn	05.45	40/45
5.5	Kidlington	09.05	50
7.6	Bletchington	11.30	
9.5	Tackley	13.40	53
11.7	Heyford	16.05	55
14.6	Fritwell	19.15	56
16.8	Aynho	21.35	60
17.6	Aynho Junction	22.20	
19.2	Kings Sutton	24.00	58/sigs
22.7	**Banbury**	**30.00**	

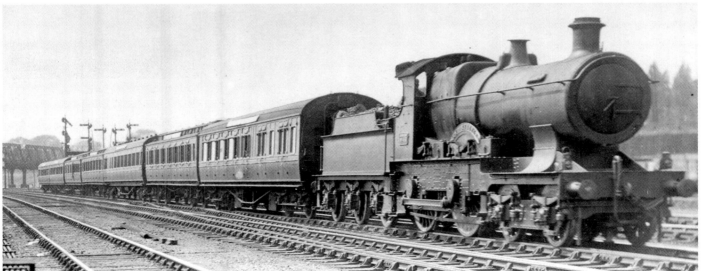

3714 *City of Gloucester* on an up stopping train at Reading 26 September 1925. (J.M. Bentley Collection)

3715 *City of Hereford* passing Kensal Green with an express from Worcester, c.1925. (GW Trust)

3719 *City of Exeter* on an up freight near Goring, c.1927. (GW Trust)

3710 *City of Bath* taking water at Shrewsbury with a stopping train for Chester, c.1925. (GW Trust)

CHAPTER 6

THE 'FLOWERS'

DESIGN & CONSTRUCTION

By 1908, Churchward's construction of his 'standard' designs, including his 4-6-0s, was well underway and he already had in addition twenty 'Badminton', forty 'Atbara' and ten 'City' double-framed 4-4-0s and twenty 'County' 4-4-0s in traffic. He had equipped some of the 'Atbaras' with Swindon No.4 boilers, although he would soon make a decision to replace these with lighter No.2 boilers as their frames were showing already excessive wear under the heavy boilers. Six of the later 'Atbaras' in the 3400 series had also been equipped with No.4 boilers following the provision of the first on 3405 back in 1902 and were being brought into line with the 'City' class. In the circumstances the decision of Churchward to build twenty further double-framed 6ft 8in 4-4-0s in 1908 seems a little curious.

However, the first decade of the twentieth century was a period of great expansion of the Great Western Railway, with the construction of the main line direct routes to Exeter via Westbury, South Wales via Badminton and Birmingham via Bicester. The boat traffic was developing via the enlarged Fishguard Harbour, requiring increased modern power west of Cardiff and the GW was in competition with other railways for the burgeoning passenger traffic, particularly the LNWR to Birmingham and the Midland between Bristol and Birmingham. The GW services to compete were fast and – for those years – comparatively frequent and in the build-up periods were fairly lightweight for which the fast 4-4-0s were more than sufficient, leaving the 4-6-0s to work the heavier trains to Bristol and the West of England.

Churchward therefore had a further twenty double-framed 4-4-0s constructed between May and July 1908 to cater for some of this developing traffic. They were in their basic concept identical to the successful 'Atbaras', although he took the opportunity to modernise the design from experience, in particular, providing deeper frames to strengthen the apparent weakness there of the earlier engines. He also provided screw reverse, enlarged

4107 *Cineraria* in the photograph from which the Moore painting was copied. (J.M. Bentley Collection/Real Photographs)

4102 *Begonia* as built in May 1908 in Works Grey, with copper-capped chimney and deeper frames. (GW Trust)

sandboxes, and externally the new 'Flower' class as they were named, were enhanced by the provision of copper-capped chimneys. He provided them with long-coned Standard No.2 boilers, without, at this stage, superheating or top feed. There was also a change in the bogie design, taking the experience of the De Glehn atlantics into account. Instead of the Dean suspension arrangement, Churchward modified it, later applying it to all the inside cylinder 4-4-0s and to the outside cylinder engines with bar-frame bogies. With their strengthened frames, the new engines were heavier than their predecessors.

The main differences in the dimensions of the new locomotives from the earlier inside-cylinder 4-4-0s were a reduced heating surface of 1,517.89sqft of the long cone No.2 boiler, the grate area of 20.35sqft, but boiler pressure of 195lbpsi which increased the tractive effort to 17,345lb. The engine weight was nearly two tons

heavier than the 'Atbaras' at 53 tons 6 cwt and 40 ton 3,500 gallon tenders were provided instead of 3,000 gallon tenders. Because of the standardisation of Churchward's locomotives and the inter-changeability of parts, seven of the 'Flowers' actually had short coned No.2 boilers at periods in their life, most for only a couple of years,

although one bore one for a ten year period between 1910 and 1920.

Around 1910, it was rumoured that Churchward had intended to replace the double-framed 4-4-0s even though most of them were less than a decade old. However, in the event he decided to upgrade the existing fleet equipping all of them with his taper boilers, either the No.2

4102 *Begonia* at an unidentified location, now with top feed and superheated boiler, 1911. (J.M. Bentley Collection)

or No.4. The 1908 'Flowers' were in the forefront of the superheating programme which commenced in 1910, all being completed by 1913 and top feed was provided from 1911. A new type of piston valve was fitted from 1915.

What is perhaps surprising is the light hammerblow delivered to the track by these two-cylinder 4-4-0s. The 'Saint' 4-6-0s were notoriously heavy, delivering 17.9 tons, and the outside cylinder 'County' 4-4-0s and 4-4-2Ts 16.6 tons, whereas the 'Flower', 'City' and 'Bulldog' classes all impacted just 12.9 tons, only bettered by the GW 4-cylinder 'King' many years later.

The new engines received names of flowers, rumoured to be some of Churchward's favourites from his own extensive gardens. Some of the flower types are well known but several are more obscure and some of the most popular flower names are excluded which suggests a personal selection rather than a standard PR department choice. The new engines were numbered 4101-4120, the first 4-4-0 locomotives to bear this group of numbers, though later, after the 1912 renumbering, all the 6ft 8in outside framed 4-4-0s (apart from the 'Cities') were numbered in this series, the 'Flowers' confusingly becoming 4149 to 4168 after the 'Badmintons' and 'Atbaras' but before the rebuilt 'Armstrongs'.

The names of the twenty 'Flower' class locomotives were:

4101 *Auricula*
4102 *Begonia*
4103 *Calceolaria*
4104 *Calendula*
4105 *Camellia*
4106 *Campanula*
4107 *Cineraria*
4108 *Gardenia*
4109 *Lobelia*
4110 *Petunia*
4111 *Anenome*
4112 *Carnation*
4113 *Hyacinthe**
4114 *Marguerite*
4115 *Marigold*
4116 *Mignonette*
4117 *Narcissus*
4118 *Polyanthus*
4119 *Primrose*
4120 *Stephanotis*

* (the final 'e' was dropped in 1916)

I thought that the PR department may have had some say in the choice of the second group of names until I got to *Mignonette* and again

4102 *Begonia* at Oxford, as built in 1908, seen here c.1909. (J.M. Bentley Collection)

4106 *Campanula* as built in May 1908 in ex-works condition, c.1908.
(GW Trust)

4108 *Gardenia* with top feed and Swindon No.2 superheated boiler, 1911.
(J.M. Bentley Collection/Real Photographs)

Stephanotis defeated me (I am not a gardener) but where were *Aubretia, Bluebell, Daffodil, Dahlia, Rose* or *Chrysanthemum*?

Later their copper-cap chimneys were replaced by cast iron and they were renumbered in 1912 from 4149-4168 in the same order. All the 6ft 8in double-framed 4-4-0s which had now received Swindon No.2 boilers were now known as 'Flowers' including the 'Badmintons', 'Atbaras' and rebuilt 'Armstrongs' and formed a class of seventy-three engines that worked indiscriminately on the services for which the 4-4-0s were suitable. Their livery was simplified also, the lining being simplified and the crimson

4118 *Polyanthus*, as built, showing the livery lining to good effect, c.1908. (J.M. Bentley Collection/Real Photographs)

4120 *Stephanotis*, as built, in 1908. The name of this 'Flower' had the author stumped, but according to the dictionary, 'Stephanotis' is 'a fragrant tropical climbing plant' (also sometimes known as 'Tasmanian Jasmine') – possibly in Churchward's garden? (J.M. Bentley Collection)

4164 *Mignonette* after renumbering in 1912, but with tall safety valve cover and still retaining the copper-cap chimney, c.1913. (J.M. Bentley Collection/Loco & General Publishing Co.)

4154 *Campanula* (previously 4106) with cast iron chimney, topfeed and superheated No.2 long-cone boiler, c.1925. (J.M. Bentley Collection/Photomatic)

The prototype 4149 *Auricula*, formerly 4101, seen here in final form with short safety valve cover, cast iron chimney, topfeed and superheated boiler, c.1925.
(J.M. Bentley Collection)

A detailed side view on long-cone boilered 4158 *Petunia*, seen at Leamington, c.1925.
(J.M. Bentley Collection)

underframes being replaced by black. The elaborate GWR scroll on the tender was replaced by the words 'Great Western' with the GW crest in the centre.

As stated previously, seven 'Flowers' had spells when they bore short coned taper boilers instead of the long coned boilers with which they had been built. The following locomotives were equipped with these exchanged boilers as follows:

4104: 1911-1913
4113: 1910-1912
4118: 1910-1912
4120: 1910-1912
4155: 1917-1920
4158: 1913-1916

4104 *Calendula* as built at Oxford, with one of the short-cone No.2 boilers, which 4104 carried between 1911 and 1913, c.1911.
(J.M. Bentley Collection)

4162 *Marguerite* at Salisbury, its last home depot, from where it was withdrawn in August 1929, 27 May 1929.
(J.M. Bentley Collection/H.C. Casserley)

4116 *Mignonette*, later 4165, was the locomotive fitted with a short-coned boiler for ten years between 1910 and 1920. Two 'Flowers' were fitted with ATC at the end of their lives, 4124 (built as an 'Atbara') and 4161. Four 4-4-0s built as 'Flowers' did not receive the new piston valves before they were withdrawn, 4155, 4156, 4158 and 4168.

The first three withdrawals of 4-4-0s built as 'Flowers' were 4153, 4164 and 4168 in 1927. The last four were 4154 and 4168 condemned in May 1930, 4164 in October and last of all, 4150 *Begonia* withdrawn from Didcot in April 1931.

4156 *Gardenia* in neglected condition shortly before its withdrawal from Leamington in April 1929.
(J.M. Bentley Collection)

4154 *Campanula* and 'Atbara' 4130 *Omdurman* on the Swindon dump awaiting breaking up, May 1930.
(J.M. Bentley Collection/Real Photographs)

4101 *Auricula* passing Hayes on a down express, c.1909.
(J.M. Bentley Collection)

OPERATION

When the 'Flowers' were first delivered they were allocated immediately to two of the newer GW timetable opportunities, the augmented lightweight fast service to Birmingham via the Bicester new route to challenge the LNWR via Rugby and the Irish and West Wales traffic beyond Cardiff. Coupled with the new motive power was the GW practice of using 'slip' coaches to serve intermediate stations without delaying the main service at locations like Princes Risborough, Banbury and Leamington on the Birmingham route. When the 'Badmintons' and 'Atbaras' had been similarly modernised these double-framed 4-4-0s with No.2 boilers were also used on the secondary route expresses from London to Weymouth and Worcester, and later to cross-country services from Cardiff to Salisbury, Bristol to Birmingham via Stratford-on-Avon and the North & West between Bristol and Shrewsbury via Pontypool Road and Hereford.

When the GWR inaugurated the new service between Bristol and Birmingham competing with the Midland Railway, there were initial legal challenges by the latter that culminated the GW using the Midland route between Bristol and Standish Junction and paying a toll.

4104 *Calendula* passing Hayes on an express for Oxford and Wolverhampton, c.1909. (GW Trust)

Therefore, the service started with just one Penzance-Wolverhampton through train, the new 4101 *Auricula* working the first train in both directions north of Bristol. By 1909 the problems had been sorted and the GW service was increased to three daily trains in each direction – Bristol to Birkenhead, Weston-super-Mare to Wolverhampton (with through coaches from Kingswear and Ilfracombe), and a service starting from Penzance and leaving Bristol at 4.45pm. The trains used the Filton, Westerleigh Junction route to Cheltenham, then via Honeybourne to Stratford-on-

4109 *Lobelia*, on an express, probably also at Hayes, a favourite photographers' location before the First World War and the creep of suburbia, c.1909. (J.M. Bentley Collection)

'Atbara' 3402 *Halifax* rebuilt with a 'City' boiler in December 1908, heading 'Flower' 4108 *Gardenia* on the first *Mauretania* Boat Train at Fishguard Harbour station, 30.8.1909. The second special with 4116 and 4111 is at the adjacent platform.

(J.M. Bentley Collection/LCGB)

Avon and Birmingham. The GW rostered the outside cylinder 'County' 4-4-0s as well as the 'Flowers' on these services north of Bristol and even 5ft 8in 'Bulldogs' on occasions. Logs of two 'Atbara' runs were described in Chapter 4 and a run was recorded behind 'Flower' 4157 *Lobelia* shortly after the 1912 renumbering, which ran smartly from Stratford to Birmingham, 25 miles in just under thirty-one minutes including signal

TABLE 19
Stratford-on-Avon–Birmingham Snow Hill

Distance Miles	Location	4157 *Lobelia* 125 tons		4162 *Marguerite* 190 tons	
		Time mins/secs	Speed mph	Time mins/secs	Speed mph
0.0	Stratford-on-Avon	00.00		00.00	
2.6	Wilmcote	04.57	37½	05.48	27½
8.0	Henley-in-Arden	10.26	65½	11.36	54½
11.0	Danzey	13.45		15.09	
14.8	Earlswood Lakes	18.07	50¾	19.56	46¾
17.6	Shirley	20.51	77½	22.53	70½
20.1	Hall Green	22.55	sigs	25.05	sigs
25.0	**Birmingham Snow Hill**	**30.56**		**33.08**	

checks approaching Snow Hill station. However, the load was only 125 tons, so the nine-mile 1 in 150 gradient from Bearley Junction to Earlswood Lakes was covered at an average speed of 53.3mph, a time only bettered by a larger boilered 'City' with a similar load. I have found a similar run with 4162 *Marguerite* with an extra couple of coaches and show both logs below.

The 4-4-0s west of Cardiff frequently had to resort to doubleheading over the undulating route as the train loads grew – especially the Southern Ireland boat train traffic. The *Mauretania* docked at Fishguard on 30th August 1909 and the GW ran three specials to London, one for the mails and two ten coach trains for the passengers. Both were doubleheaded by outside-framed 4-4-0s west of Cardiff and by a new 'Star' class locomotive on to Paddington. A log was recorded of the first special, with 'City' (rebuilt 'Atbara') 3402 *Halifax* leading 'Flower' 4108 *Gardenia*. The second boat train special was hauled by two 'Flowers', 4116 *Mignonette* and 4111 *Anemone* – unfortunately for the sake of this chapter this special was not timed – or if it was, no records of it still exist.

The special was taken forward from Cardiff by 4-6-0 4021 *King Edward*, and covered the 145 miles in 141 minutes 39 seconds, with the overall journey time including the engine change taking around four and a half hours instead of the five hours allowed in the working timetable.

Runs on ordinary express services were seldom recorded west of Cardiff, but O.S. Nock identified

TABLE 20
Cunard Special *Mauretania*, Fishguard-Cardiff-(Paddington), 30.8.1909

3402 *Halifax* leading 4108 *Gardenia*
10 chs, 274/310 tons

Distance Miles	Location	Time mins/secs	Speed mph	Punctuality	Comments
0.0	Fishguard Harbour	00.00		T	
3.1	Manorowen Box	07.50	23.7		2 miles 1 in 50 rising
15.7	Clarbeston Road	21.50	61 /50½	2¼ E	3 miles 1 in 110/165 up
-	Cardigan Junction	-	82/pws		
27.7	Whitland	32.44			
33.4	St Clears	38.34	58.6 (ave)		
36.8	Sarnau	42.04	58.3 (ave		
41.2	Drawbridge Jcn	47.22	10*		Bridge restriction
41.6	Carmarthen Jcn	47.57		4 E	
48.0	Ferryside	54.46	56.3 (ave)		
52.2	Kidwelly	54.46	66		
57.4	Pembrey	63.07	70		
61.3	Llanelly	66.28	71		
65.0	Loughor	69.54	pws/66		
67.0	Gowerton	72.10	60 / sig check*		
69.7	Cockett	76.55	45/19½		2 miles 1 in 50 rising
71.8	Landore	-	15*	10 E (approx)	
74.0	Llansamlet	83.30	39		1 in 106/91 up
76.3	Skewen	86.25	47/easy		
78.3	Neath	89.34	40*		
83.9	Port Talbot	95.58	52.5 (ave)		
90.6	Pyle	102.23	65		
-	Stormy Sdgs	-	45 (approx)		2 miles 1 in 93 / 79 up
96.0	Bridgend	109.04	45*	10 E	
99.8	Pencoed	113.41	52		
102.6	Llanharan	116.55	51		3 miles 1 in 138 / 126 up
105.1	Llantrisant	119.31	62		
109.5	Peterston	123.41	64		
112.2	St Fagans	126.21	60/64		
113.9	Ely	127.51	70		
116.3	**Cardiff**	**130.58**		**11 E**	

TABLE 21
(Paddington)-Cardiff-Landore-(West Wales)

4116 *Mignonette*
265 tons

Distance Miles	Location	Time mins/secs	Speed mph	Comments
0.0	Cardiff	00.00		
13.6	Llanharan	20.50	55/45	1 ½ miles 1 in 106 rising
20.3	Bridgend	27.30	70	
24.4	Stormy Sdgs	33.00	44/35	3 miles 1 in 132/163 up
32.4	Port Talbot	40.20	65/75	
	Neath	-	40*	
	Skewen	-	44/30/65	2 miles 1 in 99/88 rising
44.5	**Landore**	**56.20**		

TABLE 22
Leamington-Paddington via Bicester, 1910

Distance	Location	4110 *Petunia* 120 tons		4106 *Campanula* 120 tons		4110 *Petunia* 135 tons		4106 *Campanula* 200 tons	
		Time mins/secs	Speed mph	Time mins/secs	Speed mph	Time mins/secs	Speed mph	Time mins/secs	Speed mph
0.0	Leamington	00.00		00.00		00.00		00.00	
6.1	Southam Road	08.45		08.50	pws	08.05	60 /pws	09.20	pws
11.1	Fenny Compton	13.55	58	14.30	60	-		16.20	55
19.8	Banbury	22.25	62	22.30	68	23.30	65	25.25	60
24.9	Aynho Jcn	27.05	68	26.40	74	27.50	72	30.00	69
30.1	Ardley	32.40	57/50	31.30	65/58	33.05	64/59	35.25	59/50
33.9	Bicester	35.50	71/76	34.40	72	36.20	70	38.40	70/78
39.9	Brill	40.40	74	39.45	71	41.30	70	43.25	76
43.1	Ashendon Jcn	44.00	60*	43.00	60*	44.50	65*	46.30	60*
47.2	Haddenham	47.45	65	46.45	65	48.20	68	50.20	65
52.6	Princes Risboro'	53.20	58/56	52.15	59/57	54.35	52/48	55.50	59/56
60.8	High Wycombe	61.55	60/40*	60.45	60/40*	62.20	70/45*	64.15	60/40*
65.6	Beaconsfield	67.15	55/60	65.55	60	67.10	65	70.00	58
77.0	Northolt	77.25	67/74	-	69/76	76.30	74/80	79.15	75/80+
82.7	Park Royal	-	sigs (heavy)	80.40	sigs	81.15	72	83.50	75/sigs
87.3	**Paddington**	**93.20**	2¼ L	**88.45**	2¼ E	**88.35**	2½ E	**92.15**	1¼ L
Net times:		89½		87		86		90	

one that is worth outlining below – the final non-stop Cardiff-Swansea element of a London service, which was taken over at Cardiff by a 'Flower' 4-4-0.

The 'Flowers' were popular engines for the lightweight accelerated services from Birmingham using the new route via Bicester. With the loads in the early days, these 4-4-0s could surmount the banks in fine style, so it was unnecessary to push these fleet of foot locomotives hard downhill. *Railway Magazine* articles in 1911 highlighted locomotive performance on the newly opened route and included some runs with both inside and outside cylindered 4-4-0s as well as 'Saint' 4-6-0s. Four logs of two 'Flowers', 4106 and 4110, were published, three with the

minimum 120 ton load, one with 200 tons, all with net times of around 86-90 minutes for the 87 miles up from Leamington.

It will be noted that the recorder only noted passing times to the nearest five seconds and I have estimated maximum and minimum speeds based on the average section speeds and the gradient profile.

The 'Flowers' were equipped with superheated No.2 boilers between 1910 and 1913, also received topfeed, and were, like all other GW engines, renumbered in 1912, taking the numbers 4149-4168, consecutively following the 'Badmintons' and 'Atbaras' which took the earlier 41XX numbers, which must have caused some confusion to staff as well as train enthusiasts as the new 4101-20 'Badmintons' would have

looked very similar to the old 4101-20 'Flowers' apart from the shallower frame and curved running plate over the driving wheels of the 'Badmintons'.

As loads grew on the London-Birmingham route during the First World War, and with the increasing number of 4-6-0s available, the 'Flowers', along with the other 41XX 4-4-0s, found their work dwindling – their last express services in the early 1920s being the Weymouth and Worcester trains, although the cross-country services were their main contribution until the Collett express and mixed traffic 4-6-0s and the cascading 'Saints' and 'Stars' replaced them completely. The last 'Flower', 4150 *Begonia* survived at Didcot until April 1931, working local services to Oxford and Newbury/Winchester.

4116 *Mignonette* and 4111 *Anemone* stand at Fishguard Harbour with the empty stock of the second *Mauretania* special, waiting to draw into the platform, 30 August 1909. (GW Trust)

An enlargement of the double-headed pair on the second *Mauretania* special, 4116 *Mignonette* and 4111 *Anemone*, 30 August 1909. (GW Trust)

4101 *Auricula* on a Birmingham-Paddington express via
Bicester, c.1910. (J.M. Bentley Collection)

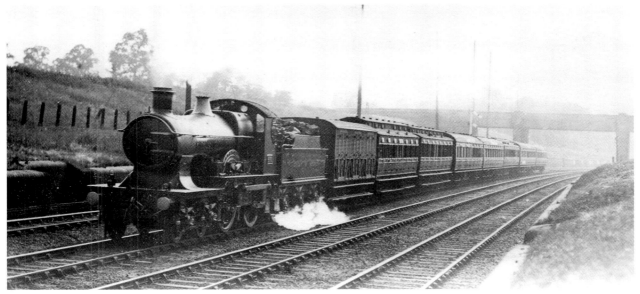

4110 *Petunia* on one of the Birmingham-Paddington lightweight fast expresses inaugurated after the opening of the Bicester cut-off, at Bentley Heath, 21 September 1910. (J.M. Bentley Collection)

4101 *Auricula* passing Bentley Heath with a Birmingham-Paddington via Bicester express, 1910. (GW Trust)

4113 *Hyacinthe* on a lightweight express in the London area, c.1910. (J.M. Bentley Collection/A.G. Ellis)

LOWER LEFT:
4112 *Carnation* shortly after rebuilding with a superheated No.2 boiler, at Paddington on a down express, possibly to Weymouth, c.1912. (J.M. Bentley Collection/Photomatic)

LOWER RIGHT:
4102 *Begonia* heads an express awaiting departure from Paddington's No.1 platform, c.1910. (GW Trust)

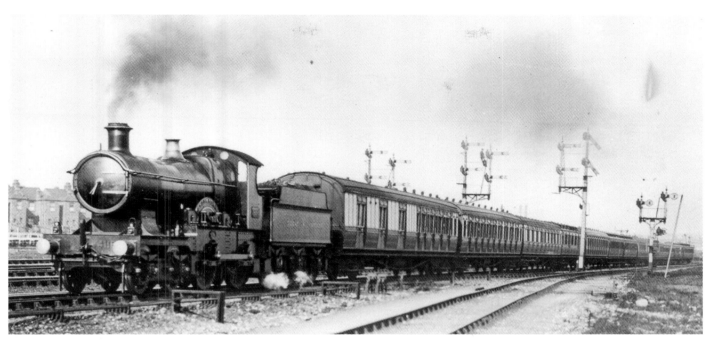

4116 *Mignonette* passes Wormwood Scrubs with a down South Wales express, c.1910. (GW Trust)

4115 *Marigold* runs alongside the estuary at Weymouth with a Paddington express, 1912. (J.M. Bentley Collection)

4155 *Cineraria* on a Birmingham-London express shortly after rebuilding with a superheated boiler in November 1911, c.1912. (J.M. Bentley Collection)

4153 *Camellia* on a Birmingham-London express at Widney Manor, c.1923. (GW Trust)

4156 *Gardenia*, with narrow cast iron chimney, on a stopping train to Reading at Hayes, c.1923. (GW Trust)

4159 *Anemone*, looking spruce despite being within eighteen months of withdrawal, near Iver with a down stopping train to Reading and Oxford, March 1928. The formation still includes some Dean 4-wheel coaches near the rear of the train. (GW Trust)

4153 *Camellia* awaiting departure from Paddington with the 2.23pm stopping train to Reading, 20 November 1924. The formation includes a number of GW 'siphons' used for conveying milk churns. (GW Trust)

4163 *Marigold* stands at Stafford Road shed with a 'Star' ready to haul a heavy 'saloon special' excursion to London, c.1913. (J.M. Bentley Collection/Real Photographs)

4158 *Petunia* approaches Oxford with a train from London, c.1925. (GW Trust)

4157 *Lobelia* on a Paddington-Birmingham express in the early 1920s. (J.M. Bentley Collection)

4155 *Cineraria* leaves Harbury Tunnel with a Birmingham-London train, c.1920.
(J.M. Bentley Collection/Loco & General Publishing Co.)

4149 *Auricula* with a Paddington-Birmingham express at Bentley Heath, July 1925. (J.M. Bentley Collection)

4149 *Auricula* at Birmingham Snow Hill with a local stopping train for Stratford-on-Avon, c.1925.
(J.M. Bentley Collection)

4152 *Calendula* at Reading with a semi-fast service for Paddington, c.1925. (J.M. Bentley Collection/K. Nunn/LCGB)

4166 *Polyanthus* at Knowle with a lightweight Birmingham-Paddington express, July 1925.
(J.M. Bentley Collection)

4166 *Polyanthus* at Knowle with a Birmingham-Stratford-Cheltenham train, c.1927.
(J.M. Bentley Collection)

4164 *Mignonette* with a Cardiff-Southampton service at Patchway, c.1925. (GW Trust)

4151 *Calceolaria* climbs Hatton Bank with a mixed freight shortly before its withdrawal in 1927. (GW Trust)

CHAPTER 7

PRESERVATION – 'CITY OF TRURO'

3440 *City of Truro* was built at Swindon in May 1903 and allocated to Exeter, from which depot it took part in the Ocean Mail specials of 1904 which sealed its celebrity status. It was superheated in November 1911 and renumbered 3717 in the GWR scheme of 1912. After twenty-eight years' life, and running up 1,081,101 miles in service, it was withdrawn from Shrewsbury depot in March 1931, the penultimate member of the class in traffic, and – thanks to the efforts of Chief Mechanical Engineer, Charles Collett – found a place in the old York Railway Museum amidst preserved engines of the former North Eastern and Great Northern Railway Companies.

After evacuation to the Scottish border country during the Second World War, it returned to the LNER Museum at York. Then, at the beginning of 1957, now acknowledged as part of the national collection, it was removed from the museum and taken to Swindon Works, where it was meticulously restored to its former condition, as built in 1903. The restoration was thorough to operational standard, and the engine became a renowned

performer on a number of enthusiast railtours all over the mainland country in 1957. In between excursion duty it was used on local trains between Swindon and Bristol and on the Didcot-Newbury-Winchester services.

A change in its duties was apparent in 1958. When the author

was working as a relief clerk in the Old Oak Common Mechanical Foreman's office during the summer of 1958, 3440 was a daily visitor, arriving in the morning off a Reading-Paddington commuter service, staying on shed all day and returning on the 6.20pm Paddington-Reading in the evening,

The brand new 3440 *City of Truro* with original cast iron chimney at Westbourne Park depot, 1903. (GW Trust)

3717 at Birmingham Snow Hill, 30 August 1930. (J.M. Bentley Collection)

LOWER LEFT:
City of Truro, sporting its post 1912 number 3717 and just before withdrawal from the GW operating stock, at Birmingham Snow Hill with a local train for Leamington or Stratford-on-Avon, 30 August 1930. (J.M. Bentley Collection)

LOWER RIGHT:
3717 preserved as an exhibit in the old York Railway Museum, c.1950. (J.M. Bentley Collection)

3717 restored as 3440 and overhauled at Swindon ready for operation on BR-WR and on railtour excursions, 20 March 1957.

(MLS Collection/BR-WR)

3440 at Swindon Works alongside Castle 5066, August 1957.

(J.M. Bentley Collection)

3440 at Eastleigh with a Didcot-Southampton train, 23 May 1957.
(H.C. Casserley/J.M. Bentley Collection)

3440 approaching Eastleigh with a Didcot-Southampton train, passing a Urie S15 and an M7 0-4-4T, 28 May 1957.
(J.M. Bentley Collection/ L. Hanson)

an eight coach non-corridor set, crammed with home-going commuters. I therefore travelled one August evening out as far as West Drayton, the train's first stop. It was a dismal day of drizzle and 3440 backed onto the full BR standard non-corridor coaches in platform 5 without a glance from any of its passengers (apart from me, of course). I wondered how this veteran was going to cope with its 300 ton gross load, and sure enough, it struggled on the curve exiting the platform and wet rails, slipping several times before it got hold of the train. It then accelerated steadily, just maintaining 60mph before slowing for the West Drayton stop, in the scheduled nineteen minutes from Paddington. I wondered, however, how it would cope with the rest of the run stopping at all stations, an unsuitable job for a 6ft 8in wheeled 4-4-0 with low adhesion. The authorities eventually came to a similar conclusion and after three months, moved the engine to Didcot, where it operated more appropriately on the service from Didcot to Newbury and Winchester or on local services to Swindon, where the engine would not be overextended.

By 1959, it was again in demand for railtour duties, including a Scottish tour in combination with preserved 4-4-0 locomotives from former Scottish railway companies, although keeping

3440 on Didcot shed during its spell of working trains to Newbury, Winchester and Southampton, c.1957. (MLS Collection)

3440 piloting Churchward mogul 6313 on a *Trains Illustrated* railtour to Eastleigh, passing through Horsebridge station, 10 April 1958. (MLS Collection)

3440 at Old Oak Common between its Reading commuter turns, Summer 1958.
(David Maidment)

3440 backs onto the 6.20pm Paddington-Reading commuter service (first stop West Drayton) formed of eight non-corridor BR standard coaches – a regular duty for around three months in 1958, 16 July 1958.
(GW Trust)

in trim in the interim period on the lightweight Didcot-Winchester-Southampton trains.

After four years of continuous working, 3440 was withdrawn a second time and retired to the converted church opposite Swindon Works that was acting as the museum for GWR locomotives and artefacts. It was then repainted in plain green with black frames and renumbered 3717 and resided there until it was brought out and restored specially to participate in the 150th anniversary of the Great Western Railway in 1985.

A special pairing of 3440 with 6000 *King George V* took place on 24

3440 on its Scottish railtour duty coupled with GNSR 4-4-0 No.49, seen here at Glasgow Central before setting out for Aberdeen, 5 September 1959. (J.M. Bentley Collection)

3440 in Scotland on its 1959 tour, seen alongside double-chimney A2 60539 *Bronzino*. (GW Trust)

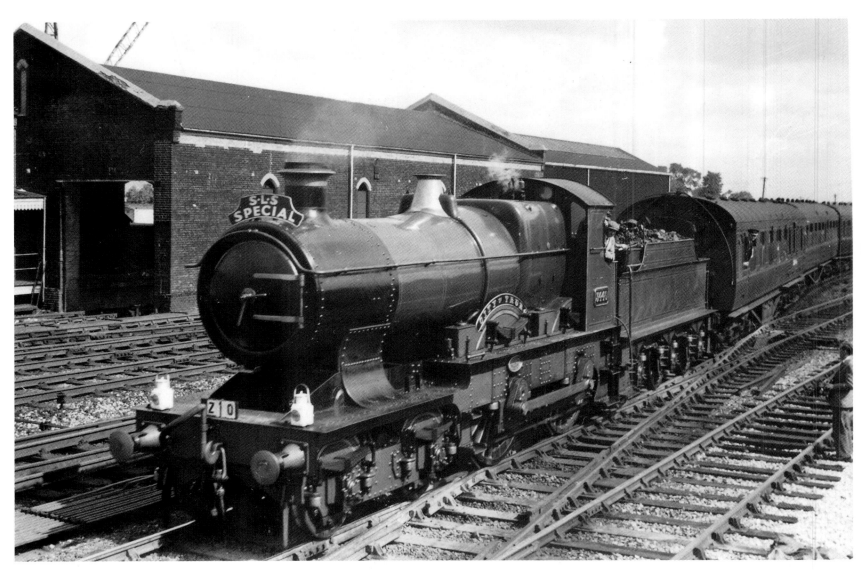

3440 brings the empty stock of an SLS special to Swindon into Southall station, 4 September 1960. (MLS Collection)

May 1986 on a heavy 13-coach *Welsh Marches Express*. The train departed London at 7.14am and left Hereford northbound twenty-two minutes late, the engines manned by Hereford crews, Drivers Prichard and Colley. Because of the weight and dimensions of the 'King', there were a number of speed restrictions imposed, between Dinmore and Ford Bridge, at Woofferton and Ludlow, and a final one to 20mph at Craven Arms, but the two engines were then worked hard to Church Stretton summit, accelerating to 50mph just after Marsh Brook and falling only to 45½mph at the summit of the 1 in 112. After a further slowing to 35mph through Church Stretton station, the pair were allowed to reach 69mph on the winding descent and reached Shrewsbury in 72 minutes 10 seconds from Hereford, just eight minutes late. The two drivers swapped footplates for the return journey, with Driver Prichard taking over 3440. The pair made a remarkable southbound run, into the teeth of a very strong westerly wind. The run was recorded by an experienced train timer, Alistair Wood, and I table above the key elements of the train's log between Shrewsbury and Hereford, where the train was taken forward to Gloucester and London by 7029 *Clun Castle*.

Alistair Wood commented that the crews had aimed to clear Church Stretton in under eighteen minutes (which they did handsomely) and that it was evident from the train that both locomotives were being worked equally hard, 3440 carrying its full share of the effort. The overall time including six service slacks must be a record with such a load.

After the year of activity, it moved to the National Railway Museum at York, and as it was still operational, was used on an occasional tour to Scarborough as part of a programme using a number of York Museum exhibits. 3440 performed its last main line railtour in May 1992and excerpts of its return from Derby to Paddington, timed by Alistair Wood, are shown in Table 24 on page 194.

It was once again given a full repair (costing £130,000) in 2004, ready to celebrate the 100th anniversary of its famous 100mph exploit and subsequently was used on a number of heritage railways, being based for a time on the Gloucester Warwick Railway at Toddington.

In 2010, 3440 was repainted once more in its original authentic livery and took part in the GW 175th anniversary events and again made visits to heritage railways, including the Llangollen Railway at their Spring Gala in 2011. However, after the need for repairs became apparent, it was withdrawn from operational activity in September 2011 and moved with other National Railway Museum exhibits to Shildon, before returning on a five year lease to STEAM Museum , to include the Swindon celebrations of 175 years as a railway town.

TABLE 23
Welsh *Marches Express*, 24.5.1986

3440 City of Truro, Driver Prichard, Hereford
6000 King George V Driver Colley, Hereford
13 coaches, 463/495

Distance Miles	Location	Time mins/secs	Speed mph	
0.0	Shrewsbury	00.00		3 L
0.8	Sutton Bridge	02.16	35	
6.5	Dorrington	09.24	56½	
10.0	MP 10	13.57	41/43	
12.0	MP 12 (Summit 1in100)	16.35	47/45½	
12.75	Church Stretton	17.48	35*	restriction
20.0	Craven Arms	25.49	60/53*/65	
22.85	Onibury	28.33	65/62	
27.5	Ludlow	35.00	33*/23*/25*	clearance restrictions
32.0	Woofferton	41.40	51	
38.5	Leominster	48.00	68/64/71	
40.8	Ford Bridge	50.06	69/59/31*	restriction
43.5	Dinmore	54.12	41/37*	restriction
46.85	Moreton-on-Lugg	57.38	63/68	
49.3	Shelwick Jcn	60.01	56	
51.0	**Hereford**	**63.20**		**15 E**

TABLE 24
Railtour, Derby – Paddington, 3.5.1992

13.50 Derby
3440 *City of Truro*
7 chs, 259/275 tons

Distance Miles	Location	Time mins/secs	Speed mph	Schedule
0.0	MP 11	00.00		50 L
7.0	Croxall	09.04	58 ½	
12.75	Tamworth	14.53	60	
14.63	Wilnecote	16.40	62	
18.25	Kingsbury	20.19	58/64	
22.4	Water Orton	22.54	66/63	
24.72	Castle Bromwich	26.28	64	
27.87	**Washwood Heath**	**30.36**		**25 L**
Track circuit failure Dorridge				
0.0	MP 118.4	00.00		25 L
2.0	Lapworth	04.41	47/pws 23*	
6.2	Hatton	12.40	38/61	
10.4	Warwick	18.08	sigs 29*	
12.4	Leamington Spa	21.42	pws 1*	
	Greaves Sidings	37.47	40/48	
23.4	Fenny Compton	42.45	53/48	
28.4	Cropredy	48.18	62/pws 25*	
32.05	**Banbury**	**55.46**		**29L**
0.0		00.00		3E
3.5	Kings Sutton	11.24	44/pws 10*	
5.14	Aynho Junction	13.43	47/41*	
9.88	Ardley	20.26	46/pws 30*	
14.04	Bicester	25.22	60	
16.88	Blackthorn	28.10	57/63	
19.88	Brill	30.11	61	
23.13	Ashendon Junction	34.36	54/65	
26.97	Haddenham	37.47	52/60	
32.52	**Princes Risborough**	**45.55**		**2 E**
0.0		00.00		3E
3.35	Saunderton	06.42	41/56	
6.2	West Wycombe	09.22	67 ½	
8.4	High Wycombe	12.42	20*	
13.35	Beaconsfield	19.25	58/32* PL	
14.7	Seer Green	21.42	54	
17.45	Gerrards Cross	24.25	64	
19.17	Denham Golf Club	25.58	68	
20.09	Denham	26.47	66 ½	
22.83	West Ruislip	29.23	59/62	
24.6	**South Ruislip**	**32.28**	**sig stand**	**1 ½ E**

Good acceleration on 3440's last main line trip. Operating delays on to Paddington reached 13 L.

3440 accelerates an NRM-sponsored
Harrogate-Scarborough excursion
out of Malton, 10 June 1986.
(MLS Collection/P.A. Michie)

3440 at Scarborough after working an excursion from Harrogate, 31 August 1987. (MLS Collection/A.C. Gilbert)

3440 poses before undertaking a railtour for the Gloucester Railway Society. (MLS Collection)

APPENDIX –
DIMENSIONS, WEIGHT DIAGRAMS & STATISTICS

Dimensions and weight diagrams are provided below for the basic designs and the most significant rebuilds of all five classes described in this book. However, because of Churchward's standardisation policy, there were frequent variations within these classes as the engines had their periodic heavy overhauls including frequent changes of boiler types affecting boiler pressure, engine weight and tractive effort. Also most engines later received higher capacity 3,500 gallon tenders, often from other withdrawn engines.

Armstrong Class

Dimensions

Cylinders:	20in x 26in
Coupled wheels:	7ft 1in
Bogie wheels:	4ft 1in
Heating surface:	1,561.33sqft
Grate area:	20.8sqft
Boiler pressure:	160lbpsi
Weight: engine:	50 tons 16 cwt
tender:	36 tons 15 cwt
total:	87 tons 11 cwt
Axleload:	15 tons 18 cwt
Tender capacity:	3,000 gallons
Tractive effort (85%):	16,640lb

As rebuilt between 1911 and 1923

As above, except:

Cylinders:	18in x 26in
Coupled wheels:	6ft 8½ in
Bogie wheels:	3ft 8in
Boiler pressure:	180lbpsi
Weight: engine:	54 tons 14 cwt
total:	91 tons 9 cwt
Axleload:	18½ tons
Tractive effort:	18,000lb

Weight Diagrams

Armstrong

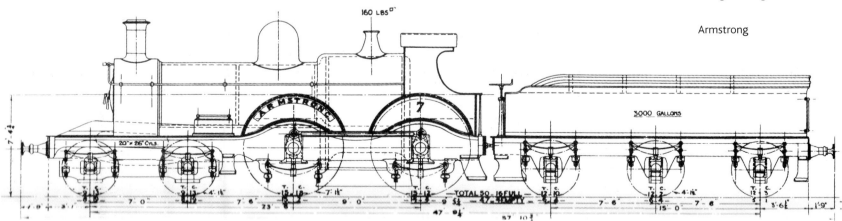

Armstrong (Churchward boiler)

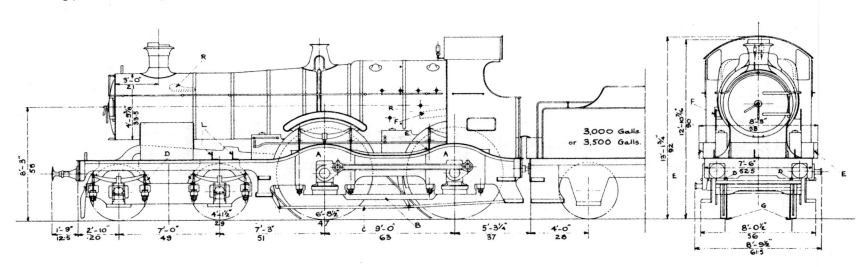

Statistics

Loco No.	Built	No.2 boiler	6' 8" wheels	Renumbered	First depot	Last depot	Withdrawn	Mileage
7	3/94	10/05	2/23	4171	Paddington	Chester	9/28	1,059,925
8	5/94	11/11	2/23	4172	Paddington	Salisbury	4/29	1,009,794
14	5/94	9/09	5/17	4170	Paddington	Bristol Bath Rd	8/28	1,070,118
16	6/94	7/09	4/15	4169	Paddington	Cardiff	7/30	1,097,920

Badminton Class

Dimensions

Cylinders:	18in x 26in
Coupled wheels:	6ft 8in
Bogie wheels:	4ft 0in
Heating surface:	1,296.9sqft
Grate area:	18.32sqft
Boiler pressure:	180lbpsi
Weight: engine:	52 tons 3 cwt
tender:	32 tons 10 cwt
total:	84 tons 13 cwt
Axleload:	15 tons 6 cwt
Tender capacity:	3,000 gallons
Tractive effort (85%):	16,010lb

3297 Earl Cawdor (F G Wright boiler)

As standard Badminton class, except:

Heating surface:	1,934.02sqft
Grate area:	17.85sqft
Boiler pressure:	210lbpsi
Weight: engine:	56 tons 14 cwt
total:	89 tons 4 cwt
Axleload:	19 tons

3310 Waterford

As above, except:

Heating surface:	1,520.03sqft
Grate area:	23.65sqft
Weight: engine:	52 tons 10 cwt
total:	85 tons

Weight Diagrams

Badminton

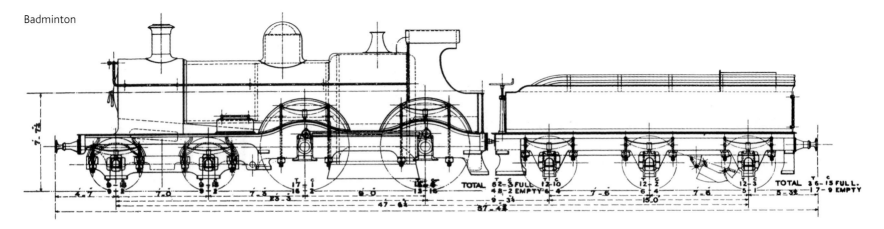

Badminton (taper boiler)

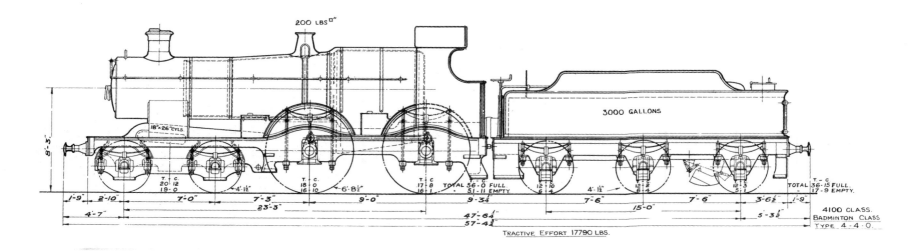

3310 Waterford

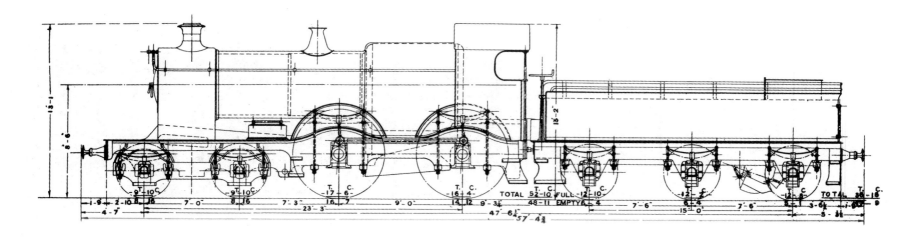

3297.Earl Cawdor

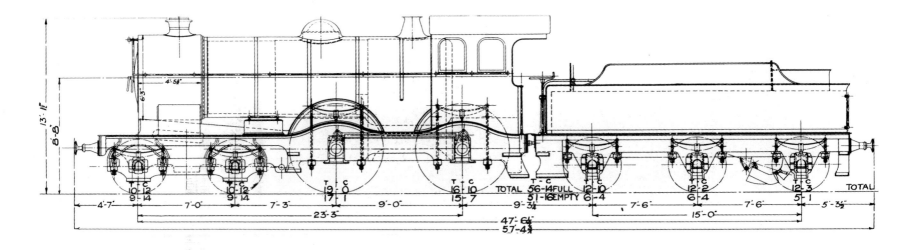

Statistics

Loco No.	Built	First depot	1912 No.	Last Depot	Withdrawn	Mileage
3292	12/97	Paddington	4100	Tyseley	9/29	1,209,489
3293	4/98	Paddington	4101	Oxford	4/30	1,107,133
3294	5/98	Paddington	4102	Tyseley	9/28	1,127,750
3295	5/98	Paddington	4103	Bristol Bath Rd	4/30	No record
3296	5/98	Bristol	4104	Cardiff	6/29	1,110,313
3297	5/98	Paddington	4105	Bristol Bath Rd	11/27	1,002,945
3298	6/98	Paddington	4106	Bristol Bath Rd	8/29	1,019,553
3299	6/98	Paddington	4107	Tyseley	2/30	1,055,868
3300	7/98	Bristol	4108	Bristol Bath Rd	3/30	1,125,734
3301	7/98	Shrewsbury	4109	Bristol Bath Rd	3/31	1,012,509
3302	7/98	Paddington	4110	Tyseley	10/28	1,006,638
3303	7/98	Bristol	4111	Oxford	10/28	1,046,250
3304	9/98	Paddington	4112	Tyseley	9/29	1,052,480
3305	9/98	Bristol	4113	Didcot	5/31	1,084,299
3306	9/98	Bristol	4114	Goodwick	7/27	1,047,016
3307	11/98	Swindon	4115	Tyseley	3/31	1,082,658
3308	12/98	Bristol	4116	Cardiff	7/27	1,036,964
3309	12/98	Bristol	4117	Bristol Bath Rd	10/27	1,007,507
3310	1/99	Bristol	4118	Bristol SPM	7/27	1,023,045
3311	1/99	Shrewsbury	4119	Didcot	7/27	932,087

Atbara Class

Dimensions

Cylinders:	18in x 26in
Coupled wheels:	6ft 8½in
Bogie wheels:	3ft 8in
Heating surface:	1,664.28sqft
Grate area:	21.28sqft
Boiler pressure:	180lbpsi (195 or 200lbs psi when fitted with No.2 coned boiler)
Weight: engine:	51 tons 12 cwt
tender:	32 tons 10 cwt
total:	84 ton 2 cwt
Axleload:	17 tons 8 cwt
Tender capacity:	3,000 gallons water, 4 tons coal (later 3,500 gallon tenders to most engines)
Tractive effort:	16,010 lb (17,345 – 17,790 lbs when fitted with No.2 boiler)

Drawing and Weight Diagram

Atbara as built with parallel boiler.

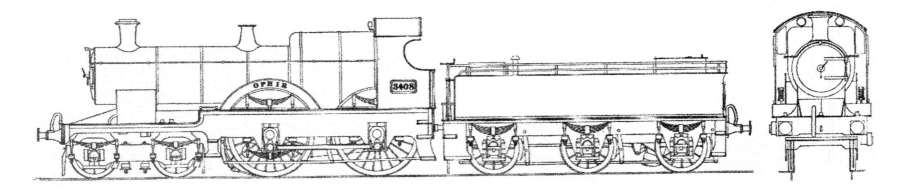

Atbara as rebuilt with Swindon No.2 tapered boiler.

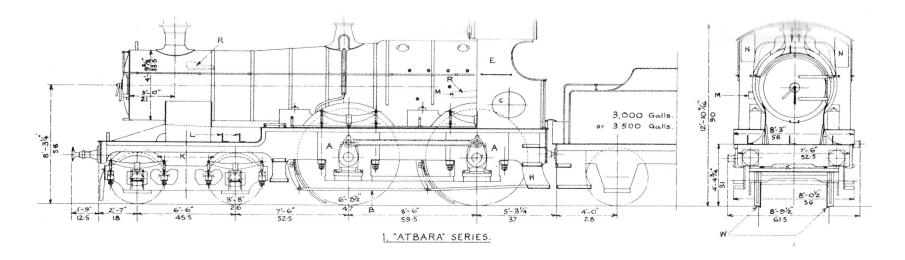

1. "ATBARA" SERIES.

Statistics

Loco No.	Built	First depot	1912 No.	Last Depot	Withdrawn	Mileage
3373	4/00	Plymouth	4120	Leamington	9/29	1,107,476
3374	4/00	Paddington	4121	Bristol Bath Rd	12/28	1,153,350
3375	4/00	Swindon	4122	Landore	10/28	939,902
3376	4/00	Exeter	4123	Cardiff	11/28	1,088,524
3377	5/00	Exeter	4124	Didcot	4/30	1,005,808
3378	5/00	Exeter	4125	Bristol Bath Rd	4/27	894,159
3379	5/00	Bristol Bath Rd	4126	Tyseley	10/27	1,031,166
3380	5/00	Exeter	4127	Tyseley	9/29	1,130,337
3381	5/00	Cardiff	4128	Swindon	7/27	1,030,337
3382	5/00	Not known	-	Not known	9/11	Accident damage
3383	7/00	Paddington	4129	Shrewsbury	11/28	1,145,282
3384	7/00	Bristol	4130	Didcot	4/30	1,061,905
3385	7/00	Bristol	4131	Cardiff	4/29	1,011,816
3386	8/00	Paddington	4132	Tyseley	4/31	1,146,700
3387	8/00	Paddington	4133	Cardiff	7/27	1,044,039
3388	8/00	Newport	4134	Cardiff	10/27	979,115
3389	8/00	Newport	4135	Bristol SPM	11/27	1,025,434
3390	8/00	Swindon	4136	Banbury	10/27	948,207
3391	9/00	Shrewsbury	4137	Westbury	10/28	948,207
3392	9/00	Paddington	4138	OOC	11/29	1,086,615
3393	6/01	Paddington	4139	Chester	9/28	969,864
3394	6/01	Exeter	4140	Salisbury	4/29	972,749
3395	7/01	Exeter	4141	Salisbury	2/30	1,078,967
3396	7/01	Plymouth	4142	Landore	10/28	956,330
3397	8/01	Stafford Rd	4143	Tyseley	4/29	1,003,776
3398	8/01	Stafford Rd	4144	Goodwick	11/27	1,000,241
3399	8/01	Paddington	4145	Westbury	12/30	1,061,832
3400	8/01	Paddington	-	Stafford Rd	Rebuilt 4/07	218,231
3401	8/01	Shrewsbury	-	Shrewsbury	Rebuilt 2/07	236,061
3402	8/01	Weymouth	-	Cardiff	Rebuilt 12/08	347,212
3403	9/01	Exeter	-	Chester	Rebuilt 2/09	286,161
3404	9/01	Bristol	-	Cardiff	Rebuilt 10/07	300,979
3405	9/01	Cardiff	-	Cardiff	Rebuilt 9/02	44,229
3406	9/01	Stafford Rd	-	Shrewsbury	Rebuilt 1/08	251,854
3407	9/01	Cardiff	-	Newton Abbot	Rebuilt 11/08	379,306
3408	10/01	Cardiff	-	Cardiff	Rebuilt 5/07	252,830
3409	10/01	Paddington	-	OOC	Rebuilt 11/07	329,307
3410	10/01	Cardiff	4146	Salisbury	10/27	877,269
3411	10/01	Weymouth	4147	Tyseley	7/27	943,106
3412	10/01	Swindon	4148	Severn Tnl Jcn	5/31	984,780

City Class

Dimensions

Cylinders:	18ft x 26in
Coupled wheels:	6ft 8½ in
Bogie wheels:	3ft 8in
Heating surface:	1.818.12sqft
Grate area:	20.56sqft
Boiler pressure:	200lbpsi
Weight: engine:	55 tons 6 cwt
tender:	36 tons 15 cwt
total:	92 tons 1 cwt
Axleload:	18½ tons
Tender capacity:	3,000 gallons (some had 3,500 gallon 40 ton tenders later)
Tractive effort: (85%)	17,790lb
Superheated:	1910 – 1912
Top feed:	From 1911
Cast iron chimneys:	From 1921

Weight Diagrams

City

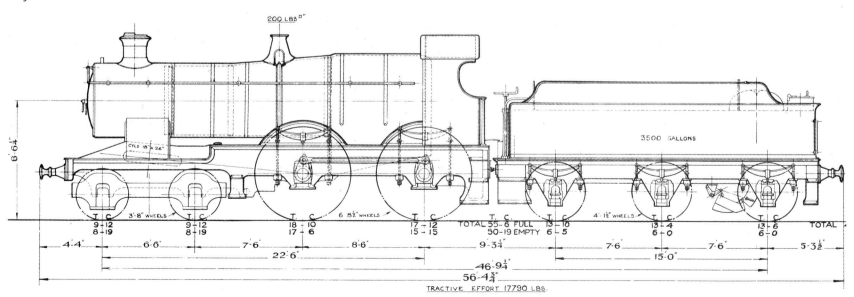

Statistics

Loco No.	Built	First depot	1912 No.	Last Depot	Withdrawn	Mileage	
3400	4/07*	Stafford Rd	3700	Stafford Road	11/29	1,007,940	
3401	2/07*	Hereford	3701	Stafford Road	8/28	837,395	
3402	12/08*	Cardiff	3702	Leamington	4/29	1,160,577	
3403	2/09*	Stafford Rd	3703	Banbury	8/29	919,931	
3404	10/07*	Cardiff	3704	Chester	9/28	999,304	
3405	9/02*	Cardiff	3705	Oxford	9/28	1,126,114	
3406	1/08*	Stafford Rd	3706	Banbury	6/29	974,312	
3407	11/08*	Newton Abbot	3707	Bristol Bath Rd	4/29	942,703	
3408	5/07*	Cardiff	3708	Shrewsbury	10/29	945,416	
3409	11/07*	OOC	3709	Oxford	9/29	1,029,344	
3433	3/03	Paddington	3710	Stafford Rd	9/28	939,181	
3434	5/03	Paddington	3711	Leamington	7/30	956,604	
3435	5/03	Bristol	3712	Reading	5/31	1,039,503	
3436	5/03	Paddington	3713	Chester	12/29	860,916	
3437	5/03	Exeter	3714	Oxford	11/29	1,107,680	
3438	5/03	Paddington	3715	Chester	10/29	1,049,705	
3439	5/03	Paddington	3716	Bristol Bath Rd	4/29	1,021,169	
3440	5/03	Exeter	3717	Shrewsbury	3/31	1,080,101	Preserved
3441	5/03	Paddington	3718	OOC	10/27	1,000,564	
3442	5/03	Exeter	3719	Oxford	4/29	783,854	

* converted from 'Atbara' by equipping with Standard No.4 ('City') boiler - for original building date, see 'Atbara' statistics

Flower Class

Dimensions

Cylinders:		18in x 26in
Coupled wheels:		6ft 8½ in
Bogie wheels:		3ft 8in
Heating surface:		1,517.89sqft
Grate area:		20.35sqft
Boiler pressure:		195lbpsi
Weight:	engine:	53 tons 6 cwt
	tender:	40 tons
	total:	93 tons 6 cwt
Axleload:		18 tons
Tender capacity:		3,500 gallons
Tractive effort (85%):		17,345lb

Weight Diagrams

Flower

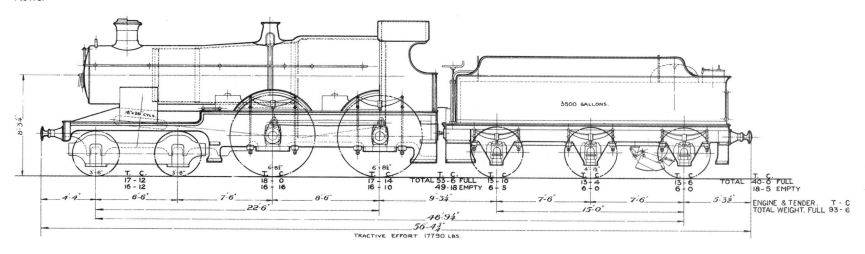

Statistics

Loco No.	Built	First depot	1912 No.	Last Depot	Withdrawn	Mileage
4101	5/08	Stafford Rd	4149	Leamington	9/29	700,682
4102	5/08	Stafford Rd	4150	Didcot	4/31	707,894
4103	5/08	Stafford Rd	4151	Pontypool	11/27	623,149
4104	5/08	Stafford Rd	4152	Bristol SPM	9/28	768,288
4105	5/08	Stafford Rd	4153	Cardiff	7/27	785,932
4106	5/08	Cardiff	4154	Tyseley	5/30	753,612
4107	6/08	Cardiff	4155	Landore	11/27	680,714
4108	6/08	Cardiff	4156	Leamington	4/29	769,697
4109	6/08	Cardiff	4157	Leamington	10/28	644,722
4110	6/08	Stafford Rd	4158	Leamington	4/29	760,698
4111	6/08	Cardiff	4159	Shrewsbury	10/29	700,532
4112	6/08	Bristol	4160	Landore	7/27	722,525
4113	6/08	Goodwick	4161	Salisbury	4/29	708,828
4114	7/08	Bristol	4162	Salisbury	8/29	743,580
4115	7/08	Bristol	4163	Cardiff	4/29	669,743
4116	7/08	Bristol	4164	Bristol Bath Rd	10/30	747,809
4117	7/08	Goodwick	4165	Salisbury	7/27	635,360
4118	7/08	Bristol	4166	Tyseley	11/27	745,005
4119	7/08	Oxford	4167	Newport	7/29	705,462
4120	7/08	Old Oak C.	4168	Taunton	5/30	743,859

BIBLIOGRAPHY

CASSERLEY, H.C. & **ASHER** L.L., *Locomotives of British Railways Great Western Group*, Andrew Dakers Ltd 1958
DRAYTON, John, *Across the Footplate Years*, Ian Allan, 1986
HOLCROFT, H., *Great Western Locomotive Practice 1837-1947*, Locomotive Publishing Company, 1957
NOCK, O.S., *Great Western 4-4-0s Part 1, Inside Cylinder Classes 1894-1910*, David & Charles 1977
NOCK, O.S., *Great Western 4-4-0s Part 2, 'Counties' to the Close 1904-1961*, David& Charles 1978
NOCK, O.S., *Fifty Years of Western Express Running*, Edward Everard Ltd, 1954
NOCK, O.S., *Four Thousand Miles on the Footplate*, Ian Allan 1952
RCTS, *Locomotives of the Great Western Parts 1-7*,
ROWLEDGE, J.W.P., *GWR Locomotive Allocations*, David & Charles 1986
RUSSELL, J.H., *Great Western Engines, A Pictorial Record*, Oxford Publishing Company 1978

INDEX